A JOHN CATT PUBLICATION

# THINKING
# READING

## WHAT EVERY SECONDARY TEACHER
## NEEDS TO KNOW ABOUT READING

**JAMES** AND **DIANNE MURPHY**

**First Published 2018**

by John Catt Educational Ltd,
12 Deben Mill Business Centre, Old Maltings Approach,
Melton, Woodbridge IP12 1BL

Tel: +44 (0) 1394 389850 Fax: +44 (0) 1394 386893
Email: enquiries@johncatt.com
Website: www.johncatt.com

**ISBN: 978 1 911382 68 3**

Set and designed by John Catt Educational Limited

# Reviews

'There is a powerful moral mission at the core of *Thinking Reading*: to ensure that no child leaves school unable to read. From the start of this important book, readers know they are in the hands of experts who can bridge the gap between extensive research and what we can do as teachers and leaders in our school contexts. We are left both informed and inspired to move beyond superficial quick fixes to reading. Essential reading for anyone involved in education.'

**Jamie Thom**
**English teacher, author of *Slow Teaching***

'This book combines passion and pragmatism – it makes a compelling case that, with the right approach, all pupils can be successful in reading, and then lays out practical steps that can help ensure teachers achieve that end. It will be a useful and motivating guide for all teachers.'

**Doug Lemov**
**MD at Uncommon Schools,**
**author of *Teach Like a Champion*,**
**Reading Reconsidered, Practice Perfect**

'I love this book! It is a call to arms to any secondary teacher who wishes to empower their students through effective reading instruction. The authors have combined a vast catalogue of research with clear, practical classroom application, employing empirically supported strategies to offer teachers a "best bet" in helping students learn to read with proficiency and pleasure.'

**Claire Hill**
**Head of English**


'Dianne and James Murphy offer us a book about the most important academic act in secondary school: reading to learn. It really is an essential aspect of learning that every secondary school teacher needs to know and understand. This book packs in an array of evidence into a compact book for busy teachers and school leaders. The "reading wars" are typically strongly contested, but Dianne and James offer a powerful voice in the debate.'

**Alex Quigley**
**English teacher,**
**director of Huntington Research School,**
**author of *Closing the Vocabulary Gap***

'James and Dianne Murphy intelligently tackle, head-on, an issue we have in secondary schools today: reading. With this book, they address the misunderstandings, the problems and the solutions as to why, and why not, students struggle to read in the classroom. Bravely, they uncover the lies and reveal to us that common strategies we use daily, weekly and termly to support students are pure snake oil. James and Dianne remove the romanticism of reading in favour of a clear, logical, reasoned and evidenced approach that speaks such common sense to teachers.

'Yes, we know reading is life-changing, but improving the process of reading needs more than an enthusiastic, cheery teacher with a love of books. To improve reading in a school, we need a better understanding of reading and how we read. A busload of enthusiastic, cheery book-loving teachers will not change a system. A busload of teachers with a better understanding of reading will change the system. Teachers need to think differently about reading and focus on their "heads" rather than their "hearts".

'*Thinking Reading* is the catalyst we need in schools today. Leaders, middle leaders and teachers need to read this if they truly want to improve students and their academic potential and success. Every child should be a reader and I feel that this book is the starting point for making sure every child will be a reader. No child should be left behind and *Thinking Reading* works hard to stop that happening.

'*Thinking Reading* is about using our heads rather than our hearts when it comes to reading in schools.'

**Chris Curtis,**
**Head of English, writer, blogger**

'An evidence-based treatise on how secondary school teachers and leaders should be approaching literacy difficulties. This book should be essential reading for all secondary school teachers to pave the way for changes to the way schools think about and plan for students who start secondary school with problems in reading and writing.'

**Alison Arrow PhD**
**Associate professor in literacy,**
**University of Canterbury, New Zealand**

'In this book, James and Dianne Murphy bring together research and teaching experience to address reading difficulties in secondary school. Secondary reading is a much-neglected topic and there is rising awareness that appropriate strategies and resources are sorely needed. *Thinking Reading* fills this gap and is essential reading for any secondary teacher who is concerned about their pupils' reading abilities but does not feel equipped to support them.'

**Dr Jessie Ricketts**
**Director, Language and Reading Acquisition laboratory,**
**Royal Holloway, University of London**

# Contents

Foreword, by David Didau ............................................................. 9

Why we wrote this book ................................................................ 13

Introduction ................................................................................. 17

Chapter 1:
Why every teacher needs to know about reading ........................... 21

Chapter 2:
Misconceptions about reading, and their consequences ................ 31

Chapter 3:
How do we learn to read, and why is it important? ....................... 49

Chapter 4:
Helping struggling readers in the secondary classroom ................ 71

Chapter 5:
What school leaders need to know and do about reading ............... 87

Chapter 6:
What does it take for effective reading intervention
at secondary school? .................................................................... 107

Afterword ..................................................................................... 129

Citations ...................................................................................... 131

Appendix: phonemic transcription chart ...................................... 141

# Foreword

Like many English teachers in secondary schools, when I embarked on my career I had, quite literally, no idea how to teach students to read. All I knew – I didn't even know this well – was how to introduce students to comprehensions strategies. When I encountered students who struggled to comprehend what they were reading I assumed this was down to them being 'less able'. And what's the point in trying to teach someone who cannot understand something? Surely that would just be cruel? So instead, I found easier texts to read to them, played games, and did what I could to cope with their increasingly poor behaviour.

One student changed my mind about much of this. In 2003 I moved to a new school and was given a 'bottom set' Year 9 group to teach. In our first lesson together I introduced myself as their new English teacher and asked each of the students to tell me something about themselves. One boy – let's call him Sam – said, 'My name's Sam, I can't read and I'm thick.'

It quickly became clear that Sam wasn't thick. His contributions in discussions were insightful and he often made interesting connections between ideas. He just couldn't read. His lived experience was that he spent his time in school going from lesson to lesson unable to do what everyone else seemed to take for granted. And as you might expect, he was deeply ashamed of this. When the pressure got too great he could become a ball of rage, and he was regularly in trouble for shouting at teachers, storming out of classrooms, and fighting with peers. He would get particularly angry when he had to go to the special needs department for one-to-one reading instruction. He hated it. He'd been doing the same things for as long as could remember and none of it made a difference.

Through a process of detective work and blind luck, I discovered that Sam almost certainly had a condition called glue ear when he started school. Glue ear is where the empty middle part of the ear canal fills up with fluid, potentially leading to temporary hearing loss. According to the NHS, an estimated 8 in 10 children suffer with undiagnosed glue ear at some time between the ages of 4 and 10. In most cases it clears up without intervention or serious consequences. But if you're unfortunate enough to have it during early reading instruction, there's a good chance you won't be able to distinguish between the different vowel and consonant sounds. While everyone else is learning how to read, glue ear sufferers are unlikely to be.

Back in 2003 there seemed to be no end of cash slopping about in the education system and I managed to get funding for Sam to be educated off site for a six-week period to receive specialist phonics instruction. He wasn't at all sure whether he wanted to do this, and worried that if *this* failed then that would be proof that he really was thick. In the end, he agreed.

Six weeks later, he came back to school a changed person. He could read. This was the most magical transformation of any student I've ever taught. He went from being an angry young man to being a model student. Suddenly he could do what everyone else could do, and, because he was bright and newly motivated to work hard, he was able to catch up. He was moved up into more academic classes and ended up leaving school with five good GCSEs, something no one had predicted. He wrote to me a few years ago to say he'd started a sports science degree at university.

Don't forget, this was a boy who couldn't read at the age of 14. The fact that he learned makes him the exception rather than the rule. It might be easy to dismiss this anecdote as depending on some special characteristic possessed by Sam, but that, I think, would be the wrong message.

Over the years since teaching Sam, I've come to realise that there are many thousands of students just like him in our schools. They are on a very predictable trajectory: most children who start secondary school unable to read fluently will leave unable to read fluently. We let ourselves off the hook for this far too readily. 'What can you do,' we console ourselves, 'with kids like that?' *It's not our fault*, after all.

True. Of course it's not our fault, but it is our responsibility. Reading difficulties are endemic, and the only chance for the vast majority of children who struggle with reading is for someone to teach them what they need to know. The only people with the necessary degree of opportunity, inclination and expertise are people who work in schools. If not us – if not *you* – then who?

That might not seem very fair. After all, if you knew how to help these children, you'd have been helping them, right? How do you even start in trying to solve such a complex, intractable problem? Happily, the Murphys are here to help!

The book you have in your hands will provide you with all the answers you need. James and Dianne Murphy have poured decades of research, thinking, hard work and practice into solving the all-too-predictable problem of teaching children in secondary schools how to read well enough to access an academic curriculum. This book is a liberation. It has the power to change lives in a very real and practical way. But be warned: once you've read it, there will no longer be any excuses for not teaching children to read.

*David Didau*
*Educational consultant, trainer and author*

# Why we wrote this book

## Dianne

'Dianne, you have to accept that you will always have children who will fail.' Even after all these years, those words still ring in my ears.

As a newly qualified teacher, I had sought advice from my tutor teacher about two six-year-olds in my bottom reading group – Simon and Justin (all pupils' names in this book are fictitious). While they were making some progress, it was slow and laboured. I had wanted advice to help me improve my practice to ensure that these boys succeeded, not to be absolved of responsibility.

At that moment, I knew that I needed to take the bull by the horns and go and find out how to teach children like these two boys. Clearly, my initial teacher training had not equipped me to do so.

Three years earlier, James had spent one year studying for a postgraduate diploma in special teaching needs. He had always said that it was something that I should do one day and that I would find it very fulfilling. Until then, I had not really given it much thought; but after receiving the above 'advice' I knew that that was exactly what I needed to do.

I applied and won a scholarship for the following year. Twenty years later I can still say that, professionally, it was the best year of my life. It was a great privilege to spend a year delving into educational research, being introduced to effective practices such as Direct Instruction, Precision

Teaching and Applied Behaviour Analysis, and being able to apply these practices in both clinical situations and classrooms.

Like other English-speaking countries, New Zealand has a long tail of underachievement in reading. When I began working as a Resource Teacher of Learning and Behaviour, collaborating with teachers in a large cluster of schools, I found that the most persistent problem I was faced with was older students who were struggling with reading. I knew that I could design programmes for these students that would help, but I was reliant on teaching assistants to deliver them. The format had to be clear, user-friendly and adaptable for each individual student. I found that when I applied those approaches I have listed above, the students made very rapid progress – quite at odds with expectations based on their prior achievement.

The programme continued to be refined and developed over the years to become what is now 'Thinking Reading'. It stands as a challenge to that opening statement, because failure in reading is not an option. It is possible to teach all students in regular schools to read well, at the same level as their peers, and therefore we have a responsibility to make sure that this happens. This book aims to support schools in that mission.

## James

When I completed my secondary teacher training in New Zealand in the early 1980s, I happened to be looking for a teaching position at the same time that many teachers were being made redundant because of falling rolls in schools. Because of the difficulty of getting a job in a school, I ended up in a variety of other jobs – a statistics clerk, an agricultural labourer, a postman. For the best part of two years I worked as a supervisor in a scheme for youth who were not merely unemployed but considered 'unemployable': no school qualifications, no work experience, no work habits, and often at the edges of the law. I quickly found that their reading and writing skills ranged from poor to very poor. In fact, the one thing they all had in common was that school had been an irrelevance to them; they had never understood what was going on in lessons and were simply waiting until they were old enough to leave.

As someone whose experience of school had been (by comparison at least) academically successful, I came to realise that my sense of 'education' had been utterly different from theirs. For me school had been a secure, rewarding, interesting place. For them, it was a nuisance that they had patiently endured. But it was the complete lack of any legacy from their school that troubled me the most. Here they were, aged 16 or more, with nothing to show for 11 years in the system – that is, 70% of their lives had been spent on something meaningless and entirely unprofitable.

The second event that changed the direction of my teaching was completing a postgraduate diploma in special teaching needs, alongside a Master of Education degree. The special teaching needs course was, unusually at that time, built upon empirical, behaviour analytic principles. Within weeks I had completely reversed many of my assumptions about teaching and learning. For years I had parroted the mantra that 'you can't measure learning'. Now I learned that observation and recording processes can be designed to ensure that I know – accurately, reliably and quickly – just how much impact my actions are having. And I learned how much has already been discovered through sound research, and what effect that could have if we could just find a way to apply it in the classroom.

Over the years I have been able to apply this learning and use it to support colleagues. Perhaps the greatest satisfaction, though, has come from seeing its application to the teaching of reading in the programme that Dianne has designed for secondary students, Thinking Reading. If my aim in education is to change lives, I can think of no better investment of my time, skill, heart and mind than in the field of reading. The power of reading to transform our view of ourselves, and our view of the world around us, makes it and it alone (as the authors of *Moral Statistics of the Highlands and Islands of Scotland* argued in 1826) 'the most effective instrument of moral improvement, without which we are as the beasts that perish'.

I want my students to live full lives, to contribute to society and to leave the world a better place than they found it. For that, they need to be able to read. This book is dedicated to that goal.

# Introduction

Nearly two centuries ago, a group of reform-minded individuals set out to transform the lives of people on the margins of Britain. They reported on their work in a book called *Moral Statistics of the Highlands and Islands of Scotland* (1826), and this is what they said about their motivation in the introduction to that work:

> The mere art of reading, ought not, perhaps, in strictness, to be held as education; yet the power which this art confers, of applying to our own use the wisdom and knowledge of every age … renders it alone the most effective instrument of moral improvement. Whether or not instruction in this art should be made universal is, we believe, no longer in debate. … Our arts and institutions, our noblest distinctions, and our most refined enjoyments – all are the gifts of education, without which, we descend almost to the level of 'the beasts that perish'.[1]

What is so important about reading? Perhaps the words of this blog post answer the question best:

> To read is to have access to the store of human knowledge. In reading we encounter not just knowledge, but the mind that recorded it, with its experiences and biases, its insights and perceptions.

---

1   Inverness society for the education of the poor in the Highlands, Inverness, Scotland. (1826). *Moral statistics of the highlands and islands of Scotland*. Inverness: Education Society.

Reading creates empathy. In reading we project ourselves into others' experiences, and come away from them changed. In reading we see past ourselves and our immediate experience; we understand the world is ever wider, and to ourselves we become ever smaller, yet ever more complex.

When I read I feed my mind and strengthen it; I use it and train it; I can grow, and compare points of view, weigh up competing ideas, and arrange the store of knowledge that reading allows me to possess. To read is to have the power to learn, regardless of the school I attend or the teacher who teaches me.

In reading I have the opportunity to master language. I hear the voices of others, and I can imitate them, blend them, and absorb them into my own voice. In reading I encounter thousands upon thousands of words I may never come across in daily speech, and with the words come thoughts and ideas I may never encounter on my own. To develop such capacities enables me to communicate in ways I could not have dreamt of without reading.

In short, reading is so essential to the transmission of culture that to be without it is to be, in every sense of the word, marginalised.

All this, of course, is agreed with by educators everywhere; we see great hand-wringing by politicians, foundations and trusts; we see sponsors lining up to support charities that seek to foster a love of reading; we see much made of reading disorders and disabilities, and much sympathy for the afflicted.

And all this is a sham. The great scandal continues, and our multi-billion-pound education system continues to churn out tens of thousands of students every year who cannot read or write adequately. What the politicians and the sponsors, by and large, do not seem to understand is what it is like to be fourteen and unable to read.

To be unable to read is to be locked out, to be isolated from discourse, to grasp the edges of conversations, to be without the knowledge of one's companions. It is to be terrified of failure, and haunted by its presence. It is humiliation and frustration, and it builds into anger, or despair. It is loneliness, and a formless sense of injustice. It is to be without the words to evince my despair.[2]

Since these words were written four years ago, we are more sure than ever that addressing the problem of adolescent illiteracy is the single most powerful, cost-effective contribution that education can make to society. This book is for the many, many children who attend secondary schools but who leave without being able to read. It is for their teachers who feel frustrated and bewildered as to why obviously intelligent children struggle with this most essential skill for learning. It is for school leaders hedged in by funding constraints and without the knowledge or time to solve the problems that poor literacy brings. And it is for those who have committed themselves to educational justice; for those who believe that no child's future should be determined by their background.

This book is also a bridge. It is our hope that through these pages you will be introduced to the power and value of good educational research, and that you will be inspired and equipped to connect with such research at a practical level – that is, at a level that benefits children and young people. Drawing upon the great body of educational research in the field of reading, we first consider why every secondary teacher needs to know about reading, and then examine the myths and misconceptions that have led to a systemic pattern of reading failure for a large proportion of our students. We explore the many skills that are required to become a good reader, how we learn to read, and the kind of support that students with reading problems at secondary school need. Finally, we offer solutions for school leaders and those who are desperate to change children's futures by solving their reading problems through effective interventions. We trust that this journey will convince you that the time and trouble required to become acquainted with effective, practical research is well worth the effort.

---

2   Murphy, J. (2014). On reading. Retrieved from horatiospeaks.wordpress. com/2014/11/23/330/.

Lastly, this book is a plea. We now have the knowledge to ensure that virtually all children can become proficient readers, yet our schools routinely fail one in five. Our hope is that you will join the growing movement for effective reading instruction for all children, regardless of social class, economic status or background – and that you will also join the work to eradicate the myths, ideologies and misconceptions that have allowed this situation to become embedded in our institutions.

# Chapter 1:
# Why every teacher needs to know about reading

*After ten years of education, Andrew was highly disruptive in lessons and was on the brink of exclusion from his secondary school. He was also reading at the level of a six-and-a-half-year-old. His levels of frustration were apparent when, asked to complete a computer-based test, he broke the mouse. He was not impressed by the thought of attending yet another reading intervention.*

*Warmth, firmness and the carrot of reading a book on football won him over, at least for the present. Andrew was smart – he had no problem with comprehension – but learning to decode the words on the page was a different matter. By his second lesson, Andrew could see that he was making progress and we had buy-in.*

*It wasn't always an easy road: Andrew had a reputation to protect with his friends, and was not always the ideal student! But he made nine years' progress in 13 months, gained five A\*–C grades in his GCSEs and became a student leader in the sixth form. At the time of writing he is completing his third year in university.*

*Not bad for a boy who 'couldn't read'.*

*Imagine how different his schooling would have been if he had been taught differently from an earlier age.*

How much do teachers need to know about reading? And why does it matter?

## Language is the door. Reading is the key

If you teach, you use language. We use language all the time and for a wide range of purposes, even if we are only dimly aware of some of these dimensions. We communicate friendship, warning, sympathy, alliance and a host of other feelings and intentions on a daily basis. Even where language seems unrewarding, we cannot help using it. Look at parents with their new babies. There is no two-way verbal conversation to be had, but that doesn't stop us talking incessantly to our newborns. We have seen teachers and carers talk constantly throughout their interactions with severely disabled people who are unable to express verbal language themselves. Language can suggest differences in levels of intimacy and social status, of warmth and distance; and the way in which others use language affects how much we feel we belong (or don't belong) to a group.

In the context of teaching, mastery of language is essential, because in addition to a myriad of social and emotional messages, we are also seeking to communicate knowledge and help our students apply that knowledge in meaningful ways. Our ability to use language for these purposes is crucial to success. And, above any other skill, we are seeking to develop our students' grasp of language, because the extent of their language skills largely determines their educational outcomes. This is why, for example, the achievement gap between rich and poor children is so stubborn: the language gap opens up early and most educational practice is not able to close it. (In fact, some educational practice can make it worse, as we shall see.)

One key body of knowledge that students need access to in order to develop their language skills is that of reading. To be clear, reading is *not* the same thing as language. We do not acquire the knowledge of how to read in the same way that we acquire our understanding and use of spoken language. Writing is a technology that humans invented just a few thousand years ago, the knowledge of which was, until the 20th century, the preserve of a minority – even in the most literate countries. In the current period, where the world is awash with information and new technologies, nearly everything is underpinned by being able to read, and to read well: exercising a wide-ranging vocabulary, a subtle grasp of syntax, a critical eye for bias, and wide background knowledge. We need this because the thinking required in our modern society is increasingly complex; and we can only make sense of our own thinking through language. Language mediates thought. If you can't think of a word for something, it's very hard to express the idea. We've seen students suddenly liberated in their writing simply from learning a few words of technical vocabulary that enabled them not only to express an idea but also to see it more clearly. And, as we shall see, reading is absolutely essential to developing language skills to the level that we need to participate in society.

This may seem obvious. But then we have to ask ourselves: if it is so obvious, why are our education systems, across the English-speaking world, producing a situation where 20% of school leavers are without the minimum reading skills they need?[3; 4] And without such skills, how are they supposed to become productive, informed and participating citizens?

Perhaps, when it comes to how we put our ideals into practice, it isn't so obvious after all. Here is our outline of why reading matters so much – and why teachers need to be, if not experts in reading, then at least very well informed.

## 1. Reading is required to access knowledge

As proficient readers, we are often unaware of how frequently we use this ability. The apparent effortlessness with which we read is why, for example, children read cereal boxes at breakfast, or passengers on commuter trains read advertisements. The process becomes so

3   Moats, L. C. (1999). *Teaching reading is rocket science*. [PDF version]. American Federation of Teachers. Retrieved from www.aft.org/sites/default/files/reading_rocketscience_2004.pdf

4   National Literacy Trust (2014). *Read on. Get on. How reading can help children escape poverty*. Save the Children on behalf of the Read On. Get On. campaign. Retrieved from literacytrust.org.uk/documents/895/Read_On_Get_On_launch_report_2014.pdf

automatic that we have taken in words and digested their meaning even before we have decided whether we want to or not. So it is easy to forget that this apparently *effortless* task is extremely *effortful* for some children.

When it comes to learning in the classroom, some students will read fluently and will quickly absorb the ideas and information that we want them to consider. Meanwhile, those for whom reading is slow, laborious and confusing will be paying so much attention to working out the words that the meaning passes them by. These students not only experience the frustration and despondency that comes from struggling with reading but also know that they have not grasped the matter that they were supposed to be learning. While they may yet absorb some of this from classroom discussion, they know that they are falling behind.

This process of falling behind continues throughout their school careers, the gap ever widening. Without ready access to the same information that other students are working with, they have an imperfect grasp of the learning. They are also distracted and discouraged by their difficulties with reading. What will be most apparent to the teacher is that the student appears to have poor recall, to be disorganised in their understanding of key information and to struggle with clearly expressing even the most basic concepts. The teacher probably thinks this student is 'low ability' – but in fact, it is not the student's intelligence but their difficulty with reading that has produced this effect. Teachers can also be misinformed by common myths that perpetuate low expectations – for example, that dyslexia is an innate neurological condition affecting otherwise able students, while poor reading is a function of low intelligence.

*Teachers need to understand the nature of reading and the implications of reading problems so that they can avoid misinterpretation of student difficulties.*

## 2. The need for good reading increases as students get older

As students progress through school, the extent to which reading is required to access the curriculum increases greatly. There is simply not enough time in lessons to teach students everything that there is to be learned. Many literature lessons, for example, rely on students having read a section of the book independently before the lesson, so that the lesson can focus on discussion of the meaning and form of the writing – not just reading it. By the time students are in upper secondary school, large chunks of textbooks, set texts in literature and other written resources will be the staple way in which information is distributed. Students who cannot read will inevitably be excluded; there will also be other students who can read, but find it effortful and unrewarding. These students will be averse to the amount of reading that is required and may avoid the task, or struggle to complete it. Inevitably, students who find reading difficult will find it harder to keep up as the amount of written information they have to process increases.

*Teachers need to understand how reading problems impact long-term curriculum progress, and what they can do about it.*

## 3. Students' negative reactions to reading can discourage teachers from providing practice, which has a compounding impact over the years

An unfortunate side effect of students struggling with large amounts of reading as they get older is that they disengage. It is natural to lose motivation for a task when it is unrewarding, and particularly so if the end result is that one feels embarrassed or humiliated by one's failure. When such students then attempt to escape the situation, to avoid the task, or to distract others from their difficulties, the teacher faces disruption. Put a number of these students in a lesson together and the level of disruption quickly escalates. As a result, teachers of students with high reading needs will often avoid providing opportunities for reading in lessons. Consequently, students progress through school with very few demands to read, but miss out on practising the very thing that they need to practise the most. The cumulative effect of this lack of practice is that students have even weaker background knowledge and are highly dependent on teachers telling them information.

*Teachers need to know how to include reading in lessons, support those with difficulty, scaffold appropriate support, and ensure regular opportunities for reading practice are planned within their curriculum.*

## 4. Students who have difficulties in reading find it increasingly hard to keep up

The student who is a poor reader faces many challenges. First, they will be discouraged by the difficulties they have. The fact that we so closely align reading and intelligence in our culture means that students almost always feel 'stupid' if they cannot read – a message that is often cruelly reinforced by their peers. Sometimes, teachers will hold a similar belief, and (perhaps unintentionally) make the message clear to the student and their classmates in all kinds of subtle and not-so-subtle ways – grouping, seating, lavish praise for a weak response, asking only the most basic questions of the student, or avoiding asking them altogether.

Students who are poor readers also face difficulties acquiring background knowledge. The student who has read a historical novel set at the end of World War Two, for example, is in a much better position to understand the topic of the Cold War than a student whose only exposure to the war is through reading about it in comics. The texts to which students are exposed in class will be much more difficult to access and remember for the student whose effort is almost totally focused on decoding the text rather than understanding it. These students will also have a much more limited vocabulary, since the great majority of less-frequent words (those beyond the most common 6000) are much more likely to be encountered in print than in speech.[5] If you can't read, you can't encounter these words unless you are explicitly taught in class. And even if you learned five new words a day for 200 days of the school year, you have only added 1000

---

5   Cunningham, A. E. & Stanovich, K. E. (2001). What reading does for the mind. *American Educator, 22*(1–2), 8–15. Retrieved from www.aft.org/sites/default/files/periodicals/cunningham.pdf

words to your vocabulary. By the end of secondary school, we need 15,000–20,000 words in our vocabulary.[6] It's virtually impossible to achieve this without proficient reading.

*If one goal of teachers is to transmit knowledge to students, then we need to understand how reading works so that we can identify and remove the barriers.*

## 5. Students with reading difficulties often develop unhelpful behaviour patterns

Consider the state of the older student who struggles with reading. Some will be drawn into a pattern of avoidance, perfecting the art of invisibility. Well behaved, quiet, and often relying on the help of a friend or two, these students will likely go through secondary school quietly falling further and further behind. Other students with reading problems will be drawn towards diverting attention away from their difficulties through disruption, performing for the amusement of their peers, humour and challenges to authority.[7] This is not to say that all disruptive behaviour proceeds from poor reading – but teachers are often surprised by how much behaviour improves when students who were previously struggling become successful readers.

*Teachers need to know about reading because it helps us to identify contributing factors to misbehaviour – behaviour that affects not only the learning of the students themselves but also that of their classmates.*

## 6. Most teachers will encounter some students with reading difficulties

Given that 20% of the general school population in English-speaking countries have reading difficulties, most teachers will encounter such students. Being able to identify their reading needs

---

6    Treffers-Daller, J. & Milton, J. (2013). Vocabulary size revisited: the link between vocabulary size and academic achievement. *Applied Linguistics Review*, 4(1), 151–172. ISSN 18686311 doi: doi.org/10.1515/applirev20130007 (Note: vocabulary estimates vary widely depending on the methodology used.)

7    Hempenstall, K. (2016). Literacy and behaviour. Retrieved from: www.nifdi.org/news-latest-2/blog-hempenstall/405-literacy-and-behaviour

and work with specialist colleagues to address these is crucial to the success of one in five of our students.[3; 4; 8]

*Teachers need to know how to provide appropriate support while specialists provide effective intervention.*

## 7. Teachers need to be able to distinguish folklore and myth from scientifically grounded practices

Even in more 'economically advantaged' areas, there is no guarantee that students will be immune to the effects of poor teaching. The key difference is that students from better-off homes are more likely to have had assessments which provide them with labels such as dyslexia, dyspraxia, or dyscalculia.[9] Invariably, these labels rely on a circular logic: the student has difficulty learning something, therefore this must be caused by a disability within the student. Having hypothesised the disability, this then becomes the explanation for the behaviour. Why can't Johnny read (or spell)? Because he is dyslexic. How do I know he is dyslexic? Because he can't read. This labelling culture in education provides an excuse for schools and teachers when we fail to teach students as they need to be taught.

*Teachers need to know about the myths surrounding reading and so-called disabilities so that they can avoid falsely lowered expectations, and target limited resources more effectively into approaches that work.*

## 8. Reading is unique in the extent to which it pervades so many aspects of students' external and internal experience

It is difficult to underestimate the extent to which reading plays a part in our everyday life. Competent reading seems so easy to the able adult reader that we find it hard to imagine how anyone could have difficulty. But, in fact, reading is not easy – particularly in English, which has a notoriously complex written (orthographic)

8   Nicholson, T. (2015, November 12). Tom Nicholson: dyslexic kids need more than kind words. *The New Zealand Herald*, Retrieved from www.nzherald.co.nz/opinion/news/article.cfm?c_id=466&objectid=11544342

9   Elliott, J. G. (2010). Dyslexia: diagnoses, debates and diatribes. *Education Canada*, 46(2), 14–17. Retrieved from www.edcan.ca/wp-content/uploads/EdCan-2006-v46-n2-Elliott.pdf

code.[10] And for a child or teenager who is growing up, forming an image of themselves and working out where they fit in society, the inability to read is a crippling affliction. Poor readers are more likely to suffer from low self-esteem and poor mental health, display more aggressive behaviour and be the victims of bullying, and tend to achieve much poorer academic outcomes at the end of schooling.[7] It is important to remember that the demands of reading are pervasive, and therefore so is the reminder that one cannot read: signs on buses, place names, directions in a hospital, the titles in a film – let alone the books and stories that students are meant to encounter 'for pleasure', the textbooks they cannot understand, the assessments that they cannot read, the request to read out loud in class and the subsequent teasing and belittling from classmates.

*Teachers need to understand the emotional, motivational and cognitive impacts of poor reading.*

## 9. There is simply nothing else in education that is able to change so many outcomes for the better, and for a relatively cheap investment

It is estimated by the National Literacy Trust that there are 6 million adults in the United Kingdom who are functionally illiterate – that is, they cannot read the front page of a newspaper, decipher the instructions on the label of a medicine bottle, or fill in a form to apply for a job.[11] Such individuals have lower earnings, poorer health, poorer housing, lower life expectancy and a much higher rate of incarceration. It is estimated that 70% of the prison population has difficulties with reading and writing. In fact, 25% of the UK prison population has reading skills at or below the level of a seven-year-old.[12] In the US, the figures are similar. Low literacy

---

10  McGuiness, D. (2004). *Early reading instruction: what science really tells us about how to teach reading.* London: MIT Press.
11  National Literacy Trust. (2017). Adult literacy. Retrieved from literacytrust.org.uk/ parents-and-families/adult-literacy/
12  Social Exclusion Unit. (2002). *Reducing re-offending by ex-prisoners.* Retrieved from www.bristol.ac.uk/poverty/downloads/keyofficialdocuments/Reducing%20 Reoffending.pdf

is estimated to cost the US economy $225 billion per year in crime, loss of productivity and lost taxes; the health costs are estimated upwards of $230 billion per year.[13] In the UK, studies have estimated the annual loss to GDP to be between £23 billion and £41 billion *per annum*, with the social cost to the country being £23 billion per year.[4; 14]

The tragedy is that this waste of human life is avoidable.[14] Schools are the places where we teach students to read, and every student but the most severely disabled can acquire this knowledge. It has been demonstrated repeatedly that even students with the most severe reading difficulties can be taught to read successfully, if given sufficiently powerful instruction.

*Teachers need to know that failure in reading is far from inevitable, and must support practices that will solve the problem at the school level.*

## 10. No child should leave school unable to read

Reading is an entitlement of every child. As a profession, and often out of the best of intentions, we have placed many barriers in the way: weak early instruction; lack of practice; incidental rather than systematic curricula; myths and misdiagnoses; tolerance of scandalous levels of reading failure; and ineffective interventions. The research is in. We know how to teach reading, and we know how to promote it at all levels of schooling. If students do not leave school reading well, it is not because of their genes, their social and economic background, or the 'bell curve'; it is because we, the teaching profession, have failed to deliver.

*Teachers need to know about reading because we have a moral obligation to ensure success in this critical skill for every child.*

---

13  National Council for Adult Learning. (2015). *Adult education facts that demand priority attention*. Retrieved from www.ncalamerica.org/AdultEDFacts&Figures1215.pdf

14  World Literacy Foundation. (2015). *The economic & social cost of illiteracy: a snapshot of illiteracy in a global context. Final report from the World Literacy Foundation.* worldliteracyfoundation.org/wp-content/uploads/2015/02/WLF-FINAL-ECONOMIC-REPORT.pdf

# Chapter 2: Misconceptions about reading, and their consequences

*'Simon will never be able to do this,' his intervention teacher said.*

*I raised my eyebrows. The 'work' in question was reading a straightforward text at a level accessible to most 12-year-olds. Simon was 14 and usually involved himself cheerfully in lessons. He was certainly working at a lower level than most of the class, but I was struck by the use of the word 'never'.*

*'He won't be able to do this,' she repeated with some fervour. 'He can't. He just can't.'*

*'Ok,' I said slowly, trying to process the bald statement with the emotional intensity behind it. 'Why can't he do it?'*

*'Because of his dyslexia,' she snapped.*

*I knew I was asking for an argument, but I asked anyway: 'How do you know he's dyslexic?'*

*She almost rolled her eyes. 'Because he can't do this!' Her exasperation was plain.*

*'So,' I said, 'let me just run over this again. He can't do it because he's dyslexic, and we know he's dyslexic because he can't do it?'*

*'Yes! So, you can't make him do it!'*

The story above is typical of conversations that we and other colleagues have had over the years. We frequently come up against a mindset that is focused on providing a disability label that justifies why a child has not learned. The reasoning behind such labels, such as in the story above, is circular. The symptoms are the justification for the label, which then becomes the explanation for the symptoms. Unfortunately, once such labels are in place, we find that there is little incentive to ensure that the child acquires the knowledge that they need to succeed. In fact, for the child to do so would be to undermine the validity of the label, so there can even be a *disincentive* to see the child make progress. As we shall see, however, it is not the child but the instruction that should be seen as deficient.

So how did we get to a place where such conversations are commonplace? Why do so many children fail in the first place?

## Disputes about reading instruction

Long ago in the 16th century, when William Shakespeare was at school, the main method of teaching reading was phonics-based. Children learned to read by connecting sounds and letters.[15] In the 19th century, when schools for the poor began to be created in earnest, large classes were often taught by poorly educated tutors through repetitive drilling and chanting. Enlightened educators, frustrated and alarmed by practices which resulted in large numbers of children knowing very little, decided to adopt what was thought to be a more sophisticated approach. The phonics code, they argued, was too difficult and unpredictable. We recognise whole words automatically when we read, so that is how learners should be taught. From the end of the 19th century to the middle of the 20th, whole-word learning ('look and say') was steadily emphasised over phonics teaching. Children's reading books were designed to give

---

15  Hempenstall, K. (2013). A history of disputes about reading instruction. Retrieved from www.nifdi.org/news-latest-2/blog-hempenstall/396-a-history-of-disputes-about-reading-instruction

large amounts of repetition for a few words at a time to aid memorisation.

The result was widespread illiteracy. In 1955, Rudolf Flesch published *Why Johnny Can't Read*,[16] a sharp critique of the standard teaching techniques of the time. Flesch argued strongly for a more phonics-based approach because it gave children much greater access to the body of knowledge that they need to decode new words as they encounter them in print. Whole-word memorisation could never meet this challenge, because each word had to be remembered individually, and the strain on the memory was too great to support learning of new words or to allow the reader to focus on comprehension.

In 1967, Jeanne Chall published *Learning to Read: The Great Debate*,[17] which aimed to settle the conflict between these two approaches. Unfortunately, despite the thorough and persuasive content of Chall's arguments in favour of phonics, the debate did not subside. Instead, a 'new' teaching approach was taking shape that seemed to have a degree of theoretical sophistication, and which chimed neatly with the anti-authority, dispense-with-conventions mood of the times. For the next four decades, an approach called 'whole language' became the dominant ideological force in the business of teaching children to read.

Before we go on, it is worth pausing to think about what is at stake here. To many, the business of teaching reading seems either basic common sense ('I learned to read OK') or an arcane kind of magic ('It's all about getting them to love books, isn't it?'). The reality is that, because reading is so integrated into every aspect of modern life, teaching reading really is equipping children for the future. It gives them a tool that they can apply independently at any time, and for a myriad of purposes. Conversely, if they are ill-equipped to read, they are lacking this essential tool whose use is required at almost every juncture of an ordinary day, from reading the captions on the morning news to understanding the instructions on a medicine bottle, to obeying street signs and following directions. Reading really is power, which means that teaching people to read is a political act.

---

16  Flesch, R. (1955). *Why Johnny can't read: and what you can do about it.* New York, NY: Harper and Row.
17  Chall, J. (1967). *Learning to read: the great debate.* New York, NY: McGraw-Hill.

The whole language proponents understood very well that the business of training teachers to teach reading is also, in many respects, a political project. The political tenets of whole language were inextricably grafted into its methodology. The language of prominent leaders of this movement, like Kenneth Goodman and Frank Smith, blended emotive arguments about freedom from authority, the autonomy of the individual, and subjective construction of reality. The scientific discourse, on the other hand, was rather thinner. The writers made assertions about the mechanics of reading that were not supported, then or later, by scientific research. The title of Goodman's influential work 'Reading: A Psycholinguistic Guessing Game' gives a broad indication of the nature of the discourse.[18; 19] Here is a (typically uncited) example from the writings of Frank Smith:

> Imagine a child reading aloud from a book. He has read five words of a sentence correctly, but now misreads the sixth. Instead of reading 'Johnny dropped the ball and ran' he reads 'Johnny dropped the ball and bat'. ... Suppose that the child was not mechanically reading one word after another, as if they had nothing to do with each other, but was trying to make sense of the entire sentence. In that case, for as far as he had got, *bat* was just as likely to be in context as *ran*, and he had made a good prediction. And if a competent reader must always rely on such predictions, or more precisely on information derived from context, then the child who made the error was doing well.[20]

Note the interpretation that incorrect reading might be as good as accurate reading. This emphasis on 'meaning first' put the child's interpretation of text at the centre of the reading phenomenon, rather than consequential to decoding the text accurately to begin with. Such arguments were then extrapolated to support the thesis that individuals each create their own meaning from text, and that the goal of instruction

---

18  Goodman, K. (1967). Reading: a psycholinguistic guessing game. *Journal of the Reading Specialist, 6*(4), 126–135. DOI: 10.1080/19388076709556976

19  Kozloff, M. (2002). A whole language catalogue of the grotesque. Retrieved from people.uncw.edu/kozloffm/wlquotes.html

20  Smith, F. (1975). *Comprehension and learning: a conceptual framework for teachers.* New York, NY: Holt, Rinehart and Winston.

should be to encourage 'making meaning' rather than allowing a particular meaning to be imposed.

While the aims of whole language proponents may have been well intended, and many of their arguments proceeded from assumptions that seemed (to them) self-evident, they were ultimately wrong. The tenets of the movement became dogmas, in the sense that they were maintained without, or even in the face of, scientific evidence.

There are three erroneous assumptions underlying the whole language 'psycholinguistic' approach:

*Erroneous Assumption 1: We learn to read in the same way that we learn to use spoken language: through continuous exposure to models and use. No systematic instruction is required (or indeed possible).*

This is erroneous because reading is not language. Reading is relating a written code to a spoken language. We do not learn to read in the same way that we learn to understand and use spoken language.

*Erroneous Assumption 2: Good readers rely heavily on context to predict words. This is what allows able readers to acquire meaning from text quickly.*

This is incorrect because, as we will discuss shortly, good readers decode text rapidly, automatically and effortlessly – so fast, in fact, that we are no longer aware of the processes being employed as we read. What seems like attention to context and visual cues is actually the luxury of thinking about what we are reading – created by the automisation of decoding.[21]

*Erroneous Assumption 3: We should teach novice readers to copy what expert readers do.*

There is no logical reason to do so, and cognitive psychology has repeatedly demonstrated that novices and experts learn quite differently. As Martin Kozloff puts it, 'fluent (automatic, effortless,

21 Stanovich, K. E. (1993). Romance and reality. *The Reading Teacher, 47*(4), 280–291. Retrieved from www.keithstanovich.com/Site/Research_on_Reading_files/RdTch93.pdf

fast and accurate) behaviour differs fundamentally from behaviour that is not fluent'.[22]

For a variety of reasons, some of them aligned to the political and social *zeitgeist* and some of them due to an almost complete absence of scientific awareness amongst teachers, whole language ideas spread rapidly and were enthusiastically endorsed. Liberated from the shackles of convention and free from the tyranny of someone else's conception of knowledge, children would now develop at their own pace, enjoy and explore books for pleasure, and find within themselves an intrinsic love of learning. Children were taught to look for context cues, including pictures, to predict (guess) and only to refer to phonic cues as a last resort, as these were considered so unreliable.

There were two main results. One group of children – those with an intuitive facility for language, from print-rich homes, with educated parents determined to do well for their children and who would not countenance reading failure – still learned to read, albeit in spite of, rather than because of, schools (but frequently with poor spelling as a legacy of this approach). Children without these supports – often poorer children, who arguably needed the opportunities created through education more than anyone else – struggled. In California, for example, one of the most dramatic adoptions of whole language across an education system was followed by a major drop in standards:

> Following the lead of Honig in California, states and districts installed whole language wholesale. In California, schools were monitored to make sure they complied with the whole language mandates and discarded whatever reading programs were in use, without regard to the performance data of children. At least three districts in California that had exceptional results using Direct Instruction were forced to drop the DI and install whole language.

> Within months after the implementation of whole language, even

---

22 Kozloff, M. A., LaNunziata, L., & Cowardin, J. (1999). *Direct instruction in education*. Retrieved from www.beteronderwijsnederland.nl/files/active/0/Kozloff%2e.a.%20DI.pdf

teachers who believed the hype and were trying to use whole language as it is specified observed that a large percentage of children were not learning to read. At the end of the first grade year, achievement test scores were significantly down.

In response to the performance of children, the states and districts issued caveats that had not been disclosed as part of the initial projections. The main assertion was that although children may be far behind at the end of kindergarten and first grade, they will catch up by the fourth grade. Exactly where the proponents of the reform got this information is not obvious. What is obvious is that many teachers told many parents, 'Oh don't worry. He'll catch up by the fourth grade.'

In the end, enough performance data was accumulated to discredit whole language completely. The data came in various forms, but mainly from achievement test performance of children in the early grades, and in Grade 4 (which revealed that the whole language promise was a fabrication). Data also came from the rising number of referrals to special classes and from the number of retentions.[23]

Well-intentioned but misguided ideas led to many children growing up struggling with reading. While the widespread adoption of whole language was creating reading failure in many English-speaking countries, researchers were pressing ahead to test the assumptions about reading that this approach was based upon.

A research bombshell was dropped on the whole language, context-based approach by Keith Stanovich and colleagues in 1981:

Fluent readers were said to have attained their skill because of a heavy reliance on context in identifying words. Reading difficulties were said to arise because some readers could not, or would not, use context to predict upcoming words.

To our surprise at the time (West and I had started these investigations

---

23 Engelmann, S. (2004). *Professional standards in education.* Retrieved from zigsite. com/Standards.htm.

thinking that the context view was correct), our initial investigations of this problem revealed just the opposite: it was the less-skilled readers who were more dependent upon context for word recognition (Stanovich, West, & Feeman, 1981; West & Stanovich, 1978).

The reason for this finding eventually became apparent: the word recognition processes of the skilled readers were so rapid and automatic that they did not need to rely on contextual information.[21]

Stanovich drily points out that, at the time, these findings 'were not warmly received' by some colleagues, but that, after repeated confirmations from multiple sources, 'scientifically, these results are now uncontroversial'. The converging findings of research showed that the ideas behind the whole language movement were entirely without scientific support. By contrast, experiments testing phonologically based theories like the Simple View of Reading[24] and Orthographic Mapping[25] have consistently endorsed and enhanced them.[26] For example, in 2017, Taylor, Davis and Rastle showed conclusively through the use of an artificial orthography that instruction in a sound-based system of reading is superior to a meaning-based approach.[27] What is true of the scientific research community is not, however, true of schools and teachers. Serious resistance to a phonics-based, systematic approach to teaching reading continues.[28]

Phonics was largely excluded from the curriculum in most English-speaking countries from the 1970s through to the early 2000s. Because of the prevalence of whole language in both schools and teacher training institutions, it is reasonable to infer that the levels of reading failure that

24  Gough, P. B. & Tunmer, W. E. (1986). Decoding, reading, and reading disability. *Remedial and Special Education*, 7(1), 1–10.

25  Ehri, L. C. (2014). Orthographic mapping in the acquisition of sight word reading, spelling memory, and vocabulary learning. *Scientific Studies of Reading*, 18(1), 5–21.

26  Kilpatrick, D. A. (2015). *Essentials of assessing, preventing, and overcoming reading difficulties*. Hoboken, NJ: John Wiley & Sons.

27  Taylor, J., David, M., & Rastle, K. (2017). Comparing and validating methods of reading instruction using behavioural and neural findings in an artificial orthography. *Journal of Experimental Psychology: General*, 20.04.2017, 1–34.

28  Moats, L. C. (2007) *Whole language high jinks: how to tell when 'scientifically-based reading instruction' isn't*. Washington, DC: Thomas Fordham Foundation.

we see in English-speaking countries are a consequence of this approach. In England, a recent estimate proposed that by age 11, 20% of children are not reading well enough to begin their secondary education.[29] In the USA, Professor Louisa Moats estimated that 'about 20 percent of elementary students nationwide have significant problems learning to read; at least another 20 percent do not read fluently enough to enjoy or engage in independent reading'.[30] In Australia, Dr Kerry Hempenstall reports:

> In a study of 3000 Australian students, 30% of 9 year olds still hadn't mastered letter sounds, arguably the most basic phonic skill. A similar proportion of children entering high school continue to display confusion between names and sounds. Over 72% of children entering high school were unable to read phonetically regular 3 and 4 syllabic words. Contrast with official figures: in 2001 the Australian public was assured that 'only' about 19% of grade 3 (age 9) children failed to meet the national standards.[31]

New Zealand, often held up as a beacon of whole language enlightenment, is the country which has exported Reading Recovery around the world – a whole language-based intervention which is intended to address the failure rates created by whole language. Respected reading researcher Bill Tunmer and his colleagues from Massey University, New Zealand, pointed out in 2013 that New Zealand had made no progress in improving literacy standards in the previous ten years, and that it continued to have the longest 'achievement tail' in the OECD – in other words, it had the largest proportion of struggling readers.[32] New Zealand was placed

29 National Literacy Trust. (2014). *Read on. Get on. How reading can help children escape poverty.* Save the Children on behalf of the Read On. Get On. campaign. Retrieved from literacytrust.org.uk/documents/895/Read_On_Get_On_launch_report_2014.pdf

30 Moats, L. C. (1999). *Teaching reading is rocket science.* [PDF version]. American Federation of Teachers. Retrieved from www.aft.org/sites/default/files/reading_rocketscience_2004.pdf

31 Hempenstall, K. (2017). Older students' literacy problems. Retrieved from www. nifdi.org/news-latest-2/blog-hempenstall/407-older-students-literacy-problems

32 Tunmer, W. E., Chapman, J. W., Greaney, K. T., Prochnow, J. E., & Arrow, A. W. (2013). *Why the New Zealand national literacy strategy has failed and what can be done about it.* Massey University Institute of Education. Retrieved from www. massey.ac.nz/massey/fms/Massey%20News/2013/8/docs/Report-National-Literacy-Strategy-2013.pdf

eighth out of nine English-speaking countries in the 2016 PIRLS survey.[33]

The result of this level of reading failure is that we have a significant percentage of students leaving secondary school unable to read at a level that will enable them to participate in society in the way that we would expect of an educated citizen. In the United Kingdom, this proportion was put at 17% by the OECD.[34] The cost to the country has been estimated at over £40 billion *per annum*.[29] In Australia, the Grattan Institute conservatively estimated that improving PISA scores by one standard deviation would increase GDP by at least 0.25%, or $3 billion *per annum*.[35] The estimated cost of low literacy in the USA is in excess of $250 billion *per annum*.[36]

Failure on such a massive scale, one would think, would lead to wholesale reform. Instead, as is the way with ideologies, rationalisations have been produced which neatly divert the conversation away from awkward questions like 'What are our schools doing to produce this kind of failure?' towards a bewildering array of myths and labels. Just as doctrines were developed to justify an indefensible practice like preventing women from voting, so myths have been constructed in education to explain why the quality of our instruction is *not* the cause of reading failure. To write about all of these myths in detail would require a large book in itself. For now, here are ten of the most common misconceptions about teaching adolescents to read.

---

33  McGrane, J., Stiff, J., Baird, J., Lenkeit, J., & Hopfenbeck, T. (2017). *Progress in international reading literacy study (PIRLS): national report for England.* Department for Education. Retrieved from www.gov.uk/government/uploads/system/uploads/attachment_data/file/664562/PIRLS_2016_National_Report_for_England-_BRANDED.pdf

34  Department for Education. (2015). *Reading: the next steps.* Retrieved from www.gov.uk/government/uploads/system/uploads/attachment_data/file/409409/Reading_the_next_steps.pdf

35  Goss, P. & Sonnemann, J. (2016). *Widening gaps: what NAPLAN tells us about student progress.* Carlton, VIC: Grattan Institute. Retrieved from grattan.edu.au/report/widening-gaps/

36  Kirsch, I. S., Jungeblut, A., Jenkins, L., & Kolstad, A. (2002). *Adult literacy in America: a first look at the findings of the National Adult Literacy Survey.* US Department of Education. Retrieved from nces.ed.gov/pubs93/93275.pdf

## 1. If students haven't learnt to read by the time they reach secondary school, it is too late

There is a general assumption that if students haven't learnt to read by the end of primary schooling, there must be something wrong with them. Once children reach this transition, the response of schools tends to be providing additional supports to compensate for the problem, rather than working towards students catching up. But in fact, students at this age can catch up, and can do so remarkably quickly given the right instruction. Once they have caught up, they can begin to access the curriculum in a new way – and their self-esteem, confidence and motivation rise. Instead of being trapped in failing to learn to read, they can read to learn, like their peers.

## 2. Low reading achievement equates to low intelligence

There is a strong tendency in education – as in wider society – to use reading as a proxy for intelligence. If you can read well, you are 'a brainbox', 'academic' or 'bookish'. If you are a poor reader, the labels are less friendly, and they certainly imply low intelligence. This is one of the reasons why the 'discrepancy model' of dyslexia has gained so much traction. This model posits that 'dyslexia' is an affliction where otherwise intelligent children have difficulty reading. By definition, it 'proves' that a child who cannot read is nevertheless intelligent, which is a great comfort to all involved, but does not help the child to read.[37] For students without such a label, the likelihood is that they will be considered less intelligent, both by themselves and their peers. One reason why poor readers do less well on IQ tests is that their lack of reading skills has denied them access to reading materials that would have developed their knowledge of the world. Poor reading is inevitably linked to poor writing and spelling, and so teachers often conclude that the student is 'less able'. Slow academic progress is inevitable if the key medium of reading to learn is not available to the learner. All of

---

37  Elliott, J. G. (2010). Dyslexia: diagnoses, debates and diatribes. *Education Canada*, *46*(2), 14–17. Retrieved from www.edcan.ca/wp-content/uploads/EdCan-2006-v46-n2-Elliott.pdf

these effects proceed from the same cause – which is not the child's intelligence quotient, but their exposure to poor instruction, and the lack of later remediation.[38]

## 3. Intelligence is innate and fixed

Intelligence is an important concept in our culture. Outside of academia, the nature of intelligence is rarely questioned – and is therefore a rather vague, fluid concept. Within academia, however, there are sharp differences of opinion. There are literally hundreds of definitions of intelligence in the psychological literature. If intelligence is defined as our ability to perform well on an IQ test, then, as we have seen, poor readers are at a substantial disadvantage, especially as they get older. On the other hand, if intelligence is defined as the ability to learn, then we must accept that the quality of instruction plays a significant role in the development of intelligence.

Intelligence is not fixed in the sense that IQ scores cannot change. Effective teaching can make a significant difference. In the first Direct Instruction pre-school, for example, Barbash comments:

> Confounding the belief that intelligence was hereditary, Engelmann found (and others later confirmed) that the mean IQ for the group jumped from 96 to 121 in one year – the largest IQ gains ever recorded in a group of children.[39]

In our work, we find that children previously labelled as 'slow learners' and having 'special learning needs' who are given access to effective reading instruction can very quickly display high levels of intelligence through a rapid rate of learning. The uncomfortable part of this proposition is that, if we see previously failing students

38 Stanovich, K. E. (1993). Does reading make you smarter? Literacy and the development of verbal intelligence. In H. Reese (Ed.), *Advances in child development and behavior, Vol. 24* (pp. 133–180). San Diego, CA: Academic Press. Retrieved from www.keithstanovich.com/Site/Research_on_Reading_files/Stanovich_Advances_1993.pdf

39 Barbash, S. (2012). *Clear teaching: with Direct Instruction, Siegfried Engelmann discovered a better way of teaching.* Education Consumers Foundation. Retrieved from education-consumers.org/pdf/CT_111811.pdf

learn very quickly when given systematic teaching, does this mean that the intervention is making them smarter – or had inadequate instruction *created* reading problems that prevented them from showing their intelligence?

## 4. The student has a processing deficit that prevents them from learning to read

The reification of learning problems – hypothesising a disability on the basis of what the student cannot yet do – is a very common response in schools. Inferred processing deficits are labelled 'dyslexia', 'dyspraxia', 'dyscalculia' and so on. This is not to minimise the difficulties that do arise from physical conditions. However, assuming that disabilities must exist because of reading difficulties is unwarranted and unhelpful. Unfortunately, the practice of reification is very common, and serves a number of important social functions, namely:

- It places the locus of the problem within the child, not with the instruction.

- It releases teachers and schools from accountability when a student has not learned.

- It provides an explanation for the child and their family that is understandable, and which can become part of a positive personal narrative about overcoming disability.

- It can be used to lobby for additional funding and resourcing for the student. This advocacy work assures schools and parents that they are doing their best for the child.

But while such labels may lead to additional resources, these do not guarantee that the child in question will learn to read and spell. Often we find that a child is resourced with 'additional hours' of support, but there is no requirement to use these hours in any particular way other than to 'support' the student.

Professor Julian Elliott of Durham University has estimated that while around 20% of students have a label of dyslexia, the true percentage of those with a genuine, innate difficulty is much less.[37] The students who are suffering from what Engelmann calls 'dysteachia' are 'instructional casualties'.[40] Misattribution of the cause of reading problems leads to a passive attitude that 'nothing can be done'.

In fact, there is an enormous amount that can be done, once we look beyond the masks created by the labels we ourselves have dispensed.

Dr Gay Keegan, District Senior Educational Psychologist in Hampshire, England said:

> As an applied educational psychologist I do not find the term 'dyslexia' helpful since there appears to be no unifying aetiology, identifying characteristics, prognosis or response to interventions which all people with 'dyslexia' share.

> So, rather than considering a single entity, I find it helpful to consider different reasons for reading difficulties, using a functional analysis rather than looking for a label.[41]

## 5. Some students will always need supports such as overlays or assistance given by a reader-writer

There is a wealth of research that has shown that the use of overlays and tinted lenses does not work. While it is understandable that teachers seek to use whatever adaptations will help a student, we can easily assume that what we are doing is helping because it boosts a student's confidence, or because the student tells us that they feel that they are learning more easily. After all, some might say, even a 'placebo effect' can help. But does it help enough, and does it have long-term results? Independent reviews of the research on Irlen lenses and overlays have found that they produce no significant difference in academic performance.[42]

40  Engelmann, S. (2010). Siegfried Engelmann 2: improving the quality of learning. Retrieved from childrenofthecode.org/interviews/engelmann2.htm

41  Durham Unversity. (2014). The term 'dyslexia' is unscientific and misleading and should be abandoned, according to new book. Retrieved from www.dur.ac.uk/news/newsitem/?itemno=20285

42  Hyatt, K. J. (2010). Irlen tinted lenses and overlays. *MUSEC Briefings 22.* Retrieved from auspeld.org.au/wp-content/uploads/2014/08/Irlen-Lenses-and-Overlays-MUSEC-Briefing.pdf

In *Keeping an eye on reading: is difficulty with reading a visual problem?*,[43] Kerry Hempenstall reviews the research literature on interventions based on adapted materials or equipment, and finds that there is no credible scientific evidence to support such a view. The social and psychological functions of this approach, though, are clear: the 'condition' removes the sense of failure from the student – 'it's not their fault, their eyes don't work right' – while at the same time exonerating teachers from the responsibility of addressing reading problems with properly designed instruction.

If students are taught to read independently, then of course the need for a reader-writer is removed. This is an important consideration, not only because of cost savings, but also because once the student leaves education, they will not have a reader-writer available to them in their day-to-day life. It is the role of schools to create independent, not dependent, readers.

## 6. We cannot expect weaker students to make rapid progress

Low expectations are a blight on students who have encountered difficulty with reading. Practical experience and scientific research have both demonstrated that with careful programme design, detailed assessment and achieving mastery in small steps, rates of progress can increase greatly. Teachers need to have the skills to determine whether a problem stems from a true lack of knowledge, a lack of fluency or low motivation.

As teachers, we often do not appreciate that in order to get a student to mastery, they may need a great deal of practice. Failure to provide sufficient practice opportunities, to perform tasks under time pressure, or to review previous learning systematically will create artificial ceilings, where the student's progress is not related to a lack of 'ability' but to an inadequate curriculum. In Engelmann's Direct Instruction programmes, for example, 70% of lesson time is devoted to practice of previously learned material.

---

43 Hempenstall, K. (2013). Keeping an eye on reading: is difficulty with reading a visual problem? Retrieved from www.nifdi.org/resources/news/hempenstall-blog/414-keeping-an-eye-on-reading-is-difficulty-with-reading-a-visual-problem

We need to teach to fluency, and to provide a large number of opportunities to generalise skills to new contexts, both of which imply a high practice component. When these conditions are met, 'slow learners' can become capable learners. As Carl Binder puts it: 'Thus, many so-called "learning disablities" turn out to be no more than a failure on the part of schools to provide carefully sequenced, timed practice on basic skills.'[44]

## 7. Introducing students to interesting books will motivate them to read, which will lead to them becoming more competent readers

Reading promotion schemes are almost *de rigueur* in secondary education. Most schools spend thousands every year on licences for such programmes, in addition to purchasing the books that they feature. Yet such programmes cannot help students whose reading is significantly behind.

Schools are willing to invest in such programmes because a) they are popular, and it is safe to be seen to be doing what everyone else seems to be doing; and b) they produce pages of figures and reports at the touch of a button, which can be used to demonstrate that data is being tracked and progress is being made. The irony, of course, is that if the school invested the funds in training staff instead of licensing software, greater gains could be made by all students, not just those who could already read.

In the National Reading Panel's influential USA report, the authors concluded that there is:

> insufficient support from empirical research to suggest that independent, silent reading can be used to help students improve their fluency (NICHD, 2000). ... Instead, teachers should provide opportunities for students to read aloud with some guidance and feedback.[45]

---

44 Binder, C. (1988). Precision teaching: measuring and attaining exemplary academic achievement. *Youth Policy*, 10(7), 12–15.

45 Hasbrouck, J. (2006). Drop everything and read – but how? *American Educator* 30(2). Retrieved from www.aft.org/periodical/american-educator/summer-2006/drop-everything-and-read-how

## 8. Comprehension is the only thing that matters in reading

In one sense, this is true, but facile. No one would dispute that reading is about extracting meaning from text. But this is not the same thing as saying that other aspects of reading don't count, in the same way that a cart will not get far without a horse. The processes involved in reading are complex and interactive, but the fact that this is challenging should not lead us into the error of oversimplification. In order to achieve the goal of comprehension, the skilled teacher needs to be able to teach a host of skills and have a systematic knowledge of the 'what' and 'how' of reading.

## 9. Phonics is just one way of teaching reading

While it is true that many children will learn to read regardless of the method of instruction they encounter, it is also true that no one learns to read an alphabetic code without phonic knowledge. Phonics is not sufficient in itself to teach children to read, but it is absolutely necessary. The only question is how best to teach this knowledge so that all children learn, not just those blessed with strong intuitive skills or supportive families.

## 10. In the digital age, reading is less important. Technology will compensate

In fact, the digital age has released vast quantities of written language upon the world. In Iceland, for example, the fear is that English on the internet will overwhelm the local language and cause it to die out.[46] News, reactions, opinions and personal messages are constantly shared through social media and information platforms. Even in schools, email communication between teachers and students is becoming increasingly common. In such an environment, everyday reading demands abound – and those who cannot read are not relieved of the burden but, rather, isolated from much of the discourse.

---

46 Henley, J. (2018, February 26). Icelandic language battles threat of 'digital extinction'. *The Guardian*, Retrieved from www.theguardian.com/world/2018/feb/26/icelandic-language-battles-threat-of-digital-extinction

This list is only a summary of some common ideas that limit the effectiveness of our practice and actively discriminate against improving outcomes for struggling readers. In the time-pressed curriculum that characterises secondary schools, with high-stakes exams looming ever closer, children with reading problems cannot afford to have barriers placed in their way. Yet, through poorly conceived instruction, resistance to scientific evidence, and attention to myths and misconceptions, we have traditionally made it much, much harder for these students to succeed. In fact, we have ensured that each year a large proportion fail who did not have to. In the next chapter we will look at how we learn to read, and what this tells us about how schools can help.

# Chapter 3:
# How do we learn to read, and why is it important?

*'Why did you leave school so soon?' I asked Lisa.*

*At 16, she was unemployed and without any prospect of work, having no qualifications and no work experience. She had been placed in a 'work scheme' to acquire some basic skills.*

*She shrugged. 'School just didn't make sense to me. I just sat there waiting for it to be over every day.'*

*'Is that because the teachers didn't explain things?'*

*'No,' she answered, shaking her head. 'I couldn't read what was on the board. I would copy stuff down sometimes, but I never understood it.'*

*I was to learn that most of the teenagers I worked with had had a similar experience of school.*

**Teachers need to know how we learn to read, because this enables us to:**
- correctly diagnose problems with learning, and avoid misattributions
- avoid inflicting the damage of myths and labels on children in our care

- challenge poor practice and promote effective, evidence-based practice

## How well do you remember learning to read?

Do you remember the stories that you first picked your way through? Do you remember the instructional methods that were used in class? Do you remember how you felt about learning to read?

The chances are that, if you are reading this book, you had a positive experience of reading. It may well have come to you with relative ease, and you enjoyed books and stories so much that it became a source of pleasure to you. For some children, success in reading is an important protection for their self-esteem in what is often a harsh social environment – the world of children and teenagers. For others, of course, failing to grasp the essentials of reading means that they will always be more vulnerable to such pressures – and may well develop a set of negative associations with reading, an activity that they associate with a frequent exposure to discomfort and shame.

But how well do you remember the actual process of learning to read? Can you remember realising that 'oo' could represent different sounds (*eg* 'book', 'room', 'blood', and even 'brooch')? Often, we may only recall particular successes or problems: struggling to work out a word like 'tongue', for example, or realising that 'kn' is a spelling for /n/. But it appears that most adults remember very little of learning to read, and not only because it happened early in life.

The reason for this is because we have achieved such a high degree of fluency. The processes involved in recognising a sequence of letters and matching them in our minds to the sounds in the word, the meaning of the word, its associated words and the connotations of its usage – all these take place in a split second for the fluent reader. To illustrate, let us take the example of driving a car. It is one thing to get into a car and drive it; it is another thing entirely to teach someone else a set of skills that has now become second nature. Do you remember the moment when you realised that you were changing gear automatically, and were focused on the road, not the interplay of clutch, gearstick, brake and accelerator? Suddenly, it was much less effort, less stress, and (for some) more fun. It is the same with many academic skills, including reading. Once word recognition becomes automatic, a complex web of skills drops below our threshold of consciousness. We simply no longer realise how quickly our brain is sorting, retrieving, matching and discarding irrelevant information to help us decode accurately – and, as a result, leaving us free to think about meaning as it is conveyed, not only in words, but through syntax, vocabulary, and a host of other elements that we refer to as 'style'.[47]

The capacity of the human brain to decode written text at astonishing speeds is, in a sense, miraculous. It is certainly a huge advantage to those of us who develop this ability. But it does have a potential downside for teachers that we all have to be aware of: because we are accustomed to reading easily, we forget how complex the process is. In fact, we become unconscious of the process taking place in our own minds. This has led to a number of unfortunate assumptions on the part of educators as to what is really going on when we read – and those intuitive (but erroneous) assumptions have been responsible for the reading failure of millions of children. This massive reading failure has then been explained away by convenient (but again scientifically unsupported) concepts of reading failure as a disability within the child, instead of a problem with the teaching.

In this chapter, we will look first at what solid research actually tells us about the various strands involved in the process of learning to read. In turn, this will provide a foundation for how we can improve outcomes for those students who have not yet mastered the written code.

## The alphabetic principle
We all learned the alphabet, many of us even before we started school. We use alphabetical order every day to organise and locate information. But where and when did alphabets begin?

The earliest technologies for recording information that we know of are ideograms. Ideograms are symbols which represent an object or idea.

---

47  Kilpatrick, D. A. (2015). *Essentials of assessing, preventing, and overcoming reading difficulties.* Hoboken, NJ: Wiley, p. 113.

They may or may not bear a resemblance to the physical object, but importantly, they represent the thing itself, not a word in a particular language. So, for example, ideograms could be used as prompts for oral historians or genealogists, without actually representing a specific word. A wavy line might represent a river, or a triangle shape might represent a mountain. Ideograms that bear a physical resemblance to the thing they represent are called pictograms. You can see both elements in a no-smoking sign. The red circle with the diagonal bar across it is an ideogram that represents the idea of 'no'. The fuming cigarette is a pictogram, designed to make clear what it is that is not permitted.

This sort of writing was not very practical at recording the complexity of language. A development was the Egyptian hieroglyphic system, where a hieroglyph could represent not only the thing it looked like (*eg* a duck, 'sā'), but another word that shared the same consonants (eg 'sā', the word for son).[48] This system enabled many more ideas to be recorded, so that, if one knew the words that might be represented by a symbol, one might work out the message. Another development was that of logograms – where symbols represented whole words, such as in Chinese script, or in Japanese *kanji*. Logograms can also represent parts of words, known as morphemes – a word part that conveys a specific meaning. Examples of English morphemes include the suffix '-ation' or the prefix 'pre-' – 'destiny' is what we are fated to become; 'destin*ation*' is the end point of a journey; '*pre*destin*ation*' means that the outcome of the journey is decided before it is begun.

A limitation of these systems was that they did not have the capacity to represent all the words in a language. Depicting abstract ideas and feelings, for example, could be cumbersome. To overcome such problems, an alphabetic system had to be developed where written symbols represented sounds – more specifically, the sound sequences that make up spoken words. Words are auditory symbols – a sequence of sounds that conveys meaning to other speakers of the same language. Alphabetic systems enabled the *written* symbols for these sounds to be combined

---

48  Tignor, R. L. (2011). *Egypt: a short history*. Princeton, NJ: Princeton University Press. p. 46

and recombined in as many sequences as required in order to represent spoken words. The earliest versions appear to have been developed by the Egyptians, Arabs and Hebrews, using consonantal systems where the vowels were inferred from the sequence of consonants. Around 1100 BC (or perhaps earlier), Phoenicians developed a more complex system including vowels. This system was developed further by the Greeks and later adapted by the Romans, and this Roman (or Latin) alphabet became widely used across Europe. (The word 'alphabet' derives from the first two letters of the Greek alphabet, alpha and beta. It is of course the Roman alphabetic system that you are decoding as you read this text.)[49]

Once armed with this knowledge of which symbols represented which sounds, the reader only needed to know two more crucial pieces of information:

a. the directions in which to sequence the script (for example, left to right and then down, as in English; right to left and then down, as in Arabic; or top to bottom and then to the left, as in classical Mandarin Chinese)

b. the importance of any additional marks, such as punctuation or accents

The proficient reader could now decode any written message in the language that the alphabet represented.

It is impossible to underestimate the significance of this achievement. Once humans had the technology to record speech, they could reproduce messages accurately over time and distance. For those who had access to this privileged knowledge, enormous possibilities for the business of government, trade, education, religion and even espionage appeared. For over 2000 years, this power lay in the hands of a minority within society, giving them immeasurable advantages over their fellow citizens. It is only in the last century or so that the idea of universal literacy has even been considered a possibility. In 1826, for example, in the *Moral*

---

49 McGuiness, D. (2004). *Early reading instruction: what science really tells us about how to teach reading. London: MIT Press.*

*Statistics of the Highlands and Islands of Scotland*,[50] the authors argued passionately that the liberation of mind and spirit, achievable through reading, should be available to all. At the time, the notion of universal literacy was a revolutionary idea; now, it seems obvious – except that, although the idea is no longer new, it is yet to be achieved.

A key barrier to achieving the noble aim of universal literacy is that the alphabetic principle has not always been explicitly taught when children are learning to read. For those who intuited the principle anyway, this was not ultimately a problem. They sailed, or sometimes muddled through. But for those children struggling with early reading, this vital knowledge of the alphabetic principle – that letters and combinations of letters represent the sounds of spoken language – was not taught explicitly enough. Even now it is common to hear educators and pseudo-educators (such as children's book authors) denounce the 'unreliable' complexity of English, arguing that children should just be allowed to experience the magic of books and stories. The written code for English is, in this view, unteachable – and attempting to teach it kills the love of reading.

The idea that a complex orthography means that we should put less effort into teaching it is of course contradictory. We do not, for example, suggest that, because medicine is very complex, we should therefore withhold the complexities of medical practice from doctors. If our aim is universal literacy, the answer is to get better at teaching this complex code, not to seek to bypass it.

## English Orthography

Orthography seems a forbidding word, but the term simply means the way in which the spoken language is represented in written code. Primarily, it means the way in which the spoken language is spelt.

English orthography is often described as 'opaque'. While some languages, such as Spanish and Finnish, have an almost one-to-one correspondence

---

50  Inverness society for the education of the poor in the Highlands, Inverness, Scotland. (1826). *Moral statistics of the highlands and islands of Scotland*. Inverness: Education Society.

between the letters of their alphabet and the sounds they represent, English does not. In English, we have between 44 and 46 phonemes (depending on accent and regional variations in speech), which are represented by 26 letters, or combinations of these letters. So, there can never be such a one-to-one correspondence between sounds and letters.

Secondly, the language that was in use at the time when writing was introduced to the English was Anglo-Saxon, or Old English. The alphabet used for Old English more accurately represented its spoken counterpart, but over time, with the influences of French and Latin, the spoken language itself changed. Moreover, the spoken language was now represented by a more Latin alphabet familiar to the clerks and monks who were the primary bearers of literacy skills in the medieval period. Later, significant changes to the way vowels were pronounced came along (the 'Great Vowel Shift').[51] These changes meant that many old spellings were preserved in the language despite significant changes in the pronunciation of the words; and some frequently used words preserved pronunciations that were at odds with more modern spelling conventions. Further, accents meant that some words were pronounced very differently in different parts of the country, so there were no standardised spellings until Dr Johnson began to compile his famous dictionary.

This is why we have some words that, at first sight, do not appear to make much sense – words like 'said', 'was', and 'enough', for example, are often cited to demonstrate the impossibility of teaching English spelling. Even words like 'to' are considered by some to be too irregular to teach. Our response is to go back to the alphabetic principle. If letters represent speech, then 'to' shows one way in which the /u:/ sound can be represented (see appendix on page 141 for a chart of phonemic symbols). It is not alone either. The word 'do' follows exactly the same principle, as do 'movie', 'removal', 'tomb', 'whom', 'into', 'lasso', 'onto', and 'who'. The representation of /ɒ/ by the letter 'a' is common in English: for example, 'was', 'watch', 'what', 'swamp', and 'malt'. Likewise, 'said' is not

---

51 McCrum, R., MacNeil, R., & Cran, W. (2011). *The story of English.* London: Faber & Faber.

alone: the word 'again' follows the same sound-spelling pattern. And, of course, while the 'gh' spelling for /f/ in 'enough' is common in many words, the 'ou' is a fairly common spelling for /ʌ/ as in 'country', 'rough', and 'trouble'. Once children understand that there are various ways for a sound to be represented by letters, it is simply a matter of learning the different ways. In other words, most of the confusion around spelling and decoding English orthography comes from the ways we have attempted to teach it. It is too complex for teaching via a simple set of rules; it is much more amenable to teaching in terms of what Kame'enui and Simmons call 'simple facts'.[52]

It is certainly true that English orthography is complex and opaque. The language has been influenced by other languages – most notably Old English, French and Latin, but also Greek and many others. The language has also evolved over time and across different places. In attempting to standardise the written orthography, many spellings that were logical at the time of their inclusion now seem obscure or downright treacherous.

Louisa Moats, in her excellent article 'How spelling supports reading',[53] points out that when children are taught to decode text alongside morphology and etymology, these spelling conundrums become far less opaque and instead open up the richness and history of the language. The spelling of English is complex because the history of the language is complex; but clearly, it can be mastered. If so, then it is the responsibility of all of us who consider ourselves guardians of our cultural past to ensure that the next generation has an appreciation of what the Māori people refer to as a *'taonga'* – a shared treasure that belongs to all of us.

## Phonemes and Phonemic Awareness

The discussion so far brings us to the essential nature of spoken language. We convey meaning through a shared understanding of sound combinations. Words are composed of syllables, closely linked groups of sounds that form a 'beat'; and syllables are composed of phonemes, the

---

52 Kame'enui, E. J. & Simmons, D. C. (1990). *Designing instructional strategies: the prevention of academic learning problems.* Englewood Cliffs, NJ: Macmillan.
53 Moats, L. C. (2005/06). How spelling supports reading. *American Educator, 29*(4), 12–22; 42–43. Retrieved from www.aft.org/sites/default/files/periodicals/Moats.pdf

smallest unit of sound in human speech. Consider, for example, the word 'discount'. It has two syllables, 'dis' and 'count'. Each of these syllables is composed of phonemes: 'dis' is formed by /d/ - /ɪ/ - /s/, and 'count' by /k/ - /aʊ/ - /n/ - /t/. (Notice that the diphthong /aʊ/ in the second syllable can be represented by a number of different spellings in English, in this case 'ou'.)

Another example of the difference between phonemes and syllables can be seen in the word 'straight'. It has only one syllable, or beat, which comprises the whole word. It may be tempting to think that the first phoneme in the word is 'str', but this is in fact a blend of three phonemes: /s/ - /t/ - /r/. This is followed by four letters, 'aigh', representing just one phoneme: the diphthong /eɪ/. Finally, there is another /t/ phoneme.

It is the ability to discriminate between these speech sounds (phonemes) that underlies reading. This awareness – called phonemic awareness – is required if we are to link phonemes to their letter representations (graphemes): for spelling, we select the correct sequences of letters to represent the sounds; for reading, we select the correct sounds that are represented by the written symbols. Research into people who have serious difficulties with decoding text – and with spelling – has regularly found that a lack of phonemic awareness is strongly associated with such problems.[54]

Research has also found that phonemic awareness is built by reading. At first this may seem counterintuitive, but without an alphabet to decipher, we have little need for phonemic awareness – the conscious discrimination of phonemes in speech. It is entirely possible to reproduce speech accurately without consciously discriminating between the phonemes. This is why many children who seem verbally fluent still struggle with decoding written text. They can readily engage with spoken language, but phonemic awareness has not developed as they were introduced to reading. In his excellent book *Essentials of Assessing, Preventing and Overcoming Reading Difficulties*, David Kilpatrick summarises the research on the most powerful interventions for children struggling to acquire reading. His conclusion is that those intervention systems that

---

54  Kilpatrick, D. A. (2015). *Essentials of assessing, preventing, and overcoming reading difficulties.* p. 101

pursued advanced phonemic awareness training 'aggressively' were clearly the most successful.

While phonemic awareness became a popular subject of reading research in the late '80s and '90s, its study predates this. Shephard Barbash notes that in the early 1960s, Siegfried Engelmann 'was the first to figure out that to learn to read one must first be able hear *and* manipulate the sounds that make up words'.[55] Engelmann had identified phonemic awareness as a logical prerequisite for accurate reading, and incorporated it into his programmes, long before research confirmed its importance.

Why do teachers need to know about phonemic awareness? Because phonemic awareness is a teachable skill that underlies reading. Failure to recognise learning problems in this area can lead to misattribution of the problem, from 'moderate learning difficulties', 'dyslexia' and 'auditory processing deficit' to 'visual processing deficits' and any number of variants on 'something wrong with the child' – when in fact, the problem has arisen because the teaching was not sufficiently thorough and robust to get them past the roadblock of phonemic awareness.

It is worth noting, too, that many adults have difficulties when asked to complete phonemic awareness tasks – such as identifying all the phonemes in a word which contains tricky blends like the 'str' in 'straight'. We should not assume that teachers and teaching assistants will have all the necessary discriminations they need to help children with such difficulties simply because they are adults. As Louisa Moats puts it, 'Teaching reading *is* rocket science'.[56]

## Phonic Knowledge

As we have seen, English has a complex orthography.

In English, there are many one-to-one correspondences between letters

---

55  Barbash, S. (2012). *Clear teaching: with Direct Instruction, Siegfried Engelmann discovered a better way of teaching.* Education Consumers Foundation. Retrieved from education-consumers.org/pdf/CT_111811.pdf

56  Moats, L. C. (1999). *Teaching reading is rocket science.* [PDF version]. American Federation of Teachers. Retrieved from www.aft.org/sites/default/files/reading_rocketscience_2004.pdf.

and consonant sounds. In nearly all instances of the phoneme /d/, the spelling is 'd', 'dd' or 'ed'. Likewise, nearly all instances of the phoneme /p/ are represented by the letter 'p' or 'pp'. However, all the 'vowel letters' (a, e, i, o and u) can represent more than one sound. There is not just a 'long' and a 'short' version. Consider the letter 'a', which can represent /æ/ as in 'ant', /eɪ/ as in 'baby', /ɑ:/ as in 'father', /ɔ:/ as in 'all', /e/ as in 'many' and /ɒ/ as in 'swan'.

There are many other cases where one phoneme can be spelt in many different ways. The phoneme /aʊ/ can be spelt 'ou', as in 'ouch'; or 'ow', as in 'clown'; or 'ough', as in 'plough'. Likewise, /ʃ/ can be written with 'sh' as in 'shape', 'ch' as in 'chef', 'ti' as in 'addition', or 'ci' as in 'official', to name a few examples.

There are also many instances where one spelling can represent different phonemes. For example, the spelling 'ch' can be a spelling for /tʃ/ in 'child', or /ʃ/ in 'chivalry' or /k/ as in 'chronicle'.

Such apparent inconsistencies are often cited as a reason why the English spelling code should not be taught. However, though the set of variations is large compared to many other languages, the set is still finite. Dr Kerry Hempenstall points out that English is more regular than is commonly supposed:

- English has 200,000 commonly used words (Bryson, 1990)
- A mere 100 words make up 60% of the words primary school children write.
- 300 words account for 75% of the words children write (Croft, 1997).
- English consonants are highly regular (initial 96%, final 91%)
- Vowels are highly irregular (isolated 52%, vowels linked to consonants in rimes 77%) (Treiman, Mullenix, Bijejac-Babic and Richmond-Welty, 1995).
- About 60% of the words in English running text are of Latin or Greek origin (Henry, 1997).

- Only 4% of English words are truly irregular (Kelssler and Treiman, 2001).[57]

Systematic phonics instruction begins with the most common and consistent items and gradually moves towards the more complex or infrequent. These less common words and sound-spellings can be mastered as the student increases the rate and difficulty level of their reading. Compare the demands of English with the enormous feat of memory performed by Chinese children, who must master a set of over 3000 logograms in order to be functionally literate. English orthography has its challenges, but as an alphabetic code it is still much easier to acquire than some systems.

Since the 1980s, there has been a growing consensus in the reading research community that the most reliable way to ensure competent reading for all students is ensuring that early readers have systematic teaching on how to interpret and use the written code. There is strong, replicated evidence for the necessity and power of this phonic code teaching.[58] The research does not claim that phonics is all that is needed to read; and nor, as far as the authors are aware, do any proponents of phonics teaching. But systematic phonics, which teaches children to blend and segment the sounds and letters – decoding and encoding, or reading and spelling – is an absolutely necessary precondition of effective reading teaching.

At this point some readers may find themselves with objections. After all, they may say, 'I wasn't taught to read using phonics, and I read perfectly well – in fact I love books and I want to pass this love of books on to the children I teach'.

It is certainly true that some people intuit the code more readily than others. However, this does not mean that we should not teach the code. Those who may quickly intuit it will not be disadvantaged by being exposed to more systematic teaching – as long as this teaching is properly sequenced and executed.

57 Hempenstall, K. (2017). Feel like a spell? Effective spelling instruction. Retrieved from www.nifdi.org/resources/news/hempenstall-blog/390-feel-like-a-spell

58 Dehaene, S. (2011) *The massive impact of literacy on the brain and its consequences for education*. Human Neuroplasticity and Education. Pontifical Academy of Sciences, Scripta Varia 117, Vatican City 2011. Retrieved from www.pas.va/content/dam/accademia/pdf/sv117/sv117-dehaene.pdf

Secondly, as we said earlier, it is generally difficult for us to remember how we learned to read. Not remembering learning phonic knowledge does not mean that it did not happen. Such instances of phonics instruction may have been incidental rather than systematic – it may have come from parents, or even older siblings – but if we have learned to read, we have acquired some phonic knowledge.

Thirdly, while a school's model of instruction may eschew phonics, this does not mean that parents – particularly those who are better off – will refrain from either directly teaching their children the required phonic knowledge or hiring a tutor to do so. Most parents want their children to read well because they understand that the skill is crucial to academic, social and professional success, and will do what it takes. It would be a better world if they didn't have to make such investments, because schools were making such a comprehensive success of teaching reading.

The issue for us is what constitutes effective teaching – not just how some children acquire reading. That means teaching for *all* students, not just the 60% who can intuit the code quickly, and the other 20% who may get it eventually. It also includes the 20% who currently miss out and are reading well behind others by the time they get to secondary school. We cannot justify excluding those at the lower end of the 'bell curve', simply expecting them to fail. We need to move the whole bell curve so that everyone reaches competency.[59] This is a reality that cannot be ignored if we are serious about the education system producing citizens who are equipped to participate productively in society.

## Language structure

We said that phonics is a necessary but not sufficient component of effective reading. A powerful complement to phonics teaching is explicit teaching of language structure. As with phonics, we have often left it to children to intuit this structure. This leaves those who do not have an intuitive inclination to flounder when they could be making steady progress. When Camilli, Vargas and Yurecko reviewed the findings of

---

59  Clarke, A. (2015, May 11). *Preventing literacy failure and shifting the whole bell curve up* [Video]. Retrieved from www.youtube.com/watch?v=mafVooDom8k.

the National Reading Panel's systematic review of methods of teaching reading, they found that explicit language teaching could double the impact of phonics alone. When combined with one-to-one tutoring, the effect was tripled.[60] Louisa Moats also contends that explicit language teaching is a key part of reading instruction: 'Expert teaching of reading requires knowledge of language structure at all levels. Without such knowledge, teachers are not able to respond insightfully to student errors, choose examples for concepts, explain and contrast words and their parts, or judge what focus is needed in a lesson.'[61]

Building awareness of the patterns in English word relationships is essential, but there is a wide variety of material for teachers to explore with students. For example, the suffixes '-ation' and '-ition' frequently enable a verb to become a noun. So, we have 'recognise' – 'recognition'; 'sedate' – 'sedation'; 'dispose' – 'disposition'; 'delegate' – 'delegation'; and so on. Explicitly teaching such patterns helps to make language more comprehensible and predictable for students. It also helps them to see that there is an underlying history and logic to the patterns that they are encountering. When combined with explicit etymology, this historical pattern becomes less opaque and more transparent.

We do not have to leave it to the children to work out such knowledge for themselves. It is much more efficient, and much more interesting, for students to be taught such patterns so that they can then discover more examples for themselves – now that they have been empowered to do so. Of course, this implies that teachers will need to have a substantial knowledge of these matters themselves – something that initial teacher training is well placed to provide, though its willingness to do so is questionable.[62; 63]

---

60  Camilli, G., Vargas, S., & Yurecko, M. (2003) Teaching children to read: the fragile link between science and federal education policy. *Education Policy Analysis Archives, 11*(15). Retrieved from epaa.asu.edu/ojs/article/viewFile/243/369.
61  Moats, L. C. (1999). *Teaching reading is rocket science.*
62  Seidenberg, M. (2017). *Language at the speed of sight: how we read, why so many can't and what can be done about it.* New York, NY: Basic Books.
63  Moats, L. (2003). Teaching teachers to teach reading. Retrieved from www.childrenofthecode.org/interviews/moats.htm

## Vocabulary

Vocabulary has been a matter of interest to reading researchers for a long time, but it has received much more recognition amongst rank-and-file teachers in recent years. Partly this comes down to the work of writers like Beck, McKeown and Kucan whose excellent book *Bringing Words to Life* (2013) has helped and inspired thousands of teachers.[64] In secondary schools, the work of Doug Lemov (2016) and his colleagues at Uncommon Schools has revolutionised the way that many teachers approach the classroom, including the ways in which we think about and teach vocabulary teaching.[65]

Vocabulary teaching is particularly important to those of us who are concerned about the achievement gap between students from economically disadvantaged homes and their better-off peers. Hart and Risley's famous paper 'The 30 Million Word Gap' delivered a hammer blow to any complacency we had enjoyed as a profession about the quality of teaching we deliver to poorer students.[66] They claimed that by the age of three, a student from a middle-class home background has been exposed to 30 million more words than the average child from a working-class home. While the findings have been questioned, there is no doubt from accumulated research conducted since that disadvantaged children do tend to start school well behind their better-off peers in language.[67] Vocabulary is an essential ingredient that must be addressed if schools are to close this knowledge gap.[68]

Vocabulary is obviously important for comprehension. It is no use having good decoding skills unless the words on the page hold meaning.

---

64  Beck, I. L., McKeown, M. G., & Kucan, L. (2013). *Bringing words to life: robust vocabulary instruction.* New York, NY: The Guildford Press.

65  Lemov, D., Driggs, C., & Woolway, E. (2016). *Reading reconsidered: a practical guide to rigorous literacy instruction.* San Francisco, CA: Jossey-Bass.

66  Hart, B. & Risley, T. R. (1995). *Meaningful differences in the everyday experiences of young American children.* Baltimore, MD: P H Brookes.

67  Nation, I. S. P. (undated). *A brief critique of Hart, B. & Risley, T. (1995).* LALS, Victoria University of Wellington. Retrieved from www.victoria.ac.nz/lals/about/staff/publications/paul-nation/Hart_and_Risley_critique.pdf

68  Kilpatrick, D. A. (2015). *Essentials of assessing, preventing, and overcoming reading difficulties.* p. 282.

To the extent that we know the words we are decoding, we can draw meaning from the text. We can even work out the likely meanings of some words from context. But this only works when there is a small percentage of unfamiliar words in a text. If there are too many (more than 5%–10%), reading is slow and painful, there is no experience of reward from uncovering the meaning of the passage, and the whole activity is frustrating. It is therefore very important that teachers are effective teachers of vocabulary.

Some suggest that spoken language development is a prerequisite or precursor to learning written vocabulary. However, there is a limit to how much new vocabulary we can pick up from speech alone. Cunningham and Stanovich (2001) point out the work of linguist Don Hayes, who found that lower-frequency words are many times more likely to occur in print than in speech. Good readers will often encounter new words in print, and this in turn grows our vocabulary.[69] What happens in the case of the child who is not a good reader? They read less, and they read less challenging material, so their vocabulary is not extended as quickly. As a result, the vocabulary gap between successful readers and non-readers grows. Hence the so-called 'Matthew effect', where those who have get more, and those who have less to begin with fall further behind.[70]

What all of this means is that we need to foster the use of new vocabulary across speech, reading material and students' own written work. Beck and colleagues suggest that students need to encounter a word ten times in different contexts to begin to incorporate it into their own vocabulary.[71] This requires systematic planning on the part of teachers, and not just for technical or academic words – the so-called Tier 3 group. Students need to be familiar with Tier 2 words, those that are more

---

69  Cunningham, A. E. and Stanovich, K. E. (2001) What reading does for the mind. *Journal of Direct Instruction, 1*(2), 137–149.

70  Stanovich, K. E. (1986). Matthew effects in reading: some consequences of individual differences in the acquisition of literacy. *Reading Research Quarterly, 21*(4), 360–407. Retrieved from www.keithstanovich.com/Site/Research_on_Reading_files/RRQ86A.pdf

71  Beck, I. L., McKeown, M. G., & Kucan, L. (2013*). Bringing words to life: robust vocabulary instruction.* New York, NY: The Guildford Press, p. 83

frequently encountered in print, and which enable them to express subtle and specific meanings. So, for example, Tier 3 words in mathematics at different levels might include the names of various polygons, types of numbers like 'logarithm', 'sine' and 'cosine', and specific terminology for the features differentiating different types of equations. In science, terms like 'hypothesis', 'electrolysis' and 'inertia' all have specific technical meanings. Meanwhile, Tier 2 words that might be useful across a number of subjects could include terms like 'relationship', 'revert', 'revolution', 'definition', and so on. In English literature, students need Tier 2 language to be able to make critical observations of texts: for example, comments on tone require students to be aware of the subtle shades of meaning expressed in terms like 'sardonic', 'sarcastic', 'cynical' and 'pessimistic'.

Vocabulary is also built through exposure to systematic and explicit teaching of language structure and etymology, as we saw above. Boardman *et al* call this 'additive instruction' where words with similar morphemic elements are presented and their connections considered.[72] A word such as 'piety', for example, can be connected to 'pious', 'pity', 'pitiful', 'pitiable' and, in the context of art history, '*pieta*'. Words with the prefix 'ana-' can be explored to understand the commonalities of meaning between such diverse examples as 'anachronism', 'anathema', 'anaphylaxis', and 'anaphora'.

Vocabulary is essential for successful reading, but the relationship is reciprocal: reading more builds vocabulary, and having a broader vocabulary builds reading skills. Students need exposure to challenging texts and rich oral language, and both of these need to be taught systematically and explicitly.

## Fluency and the Stages of Learning

We touched on fluency earlier, but here we look in more detail at the research on the impact of fluency on reading. Fluency should not be seen as a skill in isolation, but rather – as conceptualised by special education

---

72  Boardman, A. G., Roberts, G., Vaughn, S., Wexler, J., Murray, C. S., & Kosanovich, M. (2008). *Effective instruction for adolescent struggling readers: a practice brief.* Portsmouth, NH: RMC Research Corporation, Center on Instruction.

and Precision Teaching researchers such as White and Haring (1980),[73] Lindsley (1992),[74] Binder (1988),[75] Binder *et al* (2002)[76] and Kubina (2009)[77] – as a stage of learning. The Stages of Learning model states that as we become more proficient with knowledge and its application, we move through dimensions of expertise. The number of stages has been mooted in the literature as ranging from 4 to 14. Here we propose five stages that enable distinctions to be drawn without overly complicated definitions and descriptors.

- Acquisition – when the learner is still getting to grips with the learning but is not yet able to perform accurately

- Accuracy – when the learner is now able to reliably perform the task accurately but slowly

- Fluency – when the learner is able to perform the task accurately and at a socially valid and useful rate

- Retention – when the learner is able to retain the learning in long-term memory over an extended period of time (not just a few days)

- Generalisation – when the learner can appropriately apply what they have learned in different contexts

To put these into context, let us return to the example of driving before we look again at reading. Let's imagine that Julie is learning to drive. She is adjusting to the feel of the driver's seat, to the gear-shift sequence, to the interplay of indicating, checking the rearview mirror, and releasing the clutch while depressing the accelerator. It takes quite a few attempts

73  White, O. R. & Haring, N. G. (1980). Exceptional teaching for exceptional children (2nd ed.). Columbus, OH: Merrill.

74  Lindsley, O. R. (1992). Precision teaching: discoveries and effects. *Journal of Applied Behaviour Analysis*, 25(1), 51–57.

75  Binder, C. (1988). Precision teaching: measuring and attaining exemplary academic achievement. *Youth Policy*, 10(7), 12–15.

76  Binder, C., Haughton, E., & Bateman, B. (2002). *Fluency: achieving true mastery in the learning process*. Retrieved from bindel.verio.com/wb_fluency.org/Publications/BinderHaughtonBateman2002.pdf

77  Kubina, R. M., Kostewicz, D. E., & Lin, F. (2009). The taxonomy of learning and behavioral fluency. *Journal of Precision Teaching and Celeration*, 25, 17–27. Retrieved from cdn2.hubspot.net/hubfs/3031078/Chartlytics_April2017/Docs/kubina_taxonomy_and_fluency.pdf?t=1494006957153

before she can get the car to move off smoothly, and she cannot yet do this reliably. Julie is still at **acquisition**.

After some practice, however, the checking and moving-off sequence is followed smoothly and becomes quite reliable. At this point she has moved to the stage of **accuracy** – but you might still be very frustrated if you were stuck behind her at the traffic lights, because her performance is still too slow to cope with busy roads.

After a great deal more practice, however, Julie has now reached **fluency**. She changes gear with apparent effortlessness and barely needs to think about the appropriate gear to use: the engine note, the car's speed, and whether the car is accelerating or decelerating all provide signals that she processes faster than conscious thought. As a result, she is able to concentrate on the driving conditions, the road signs and traffic controls, and even have enough headspace ('working memory') to hold a conversation with her passenger.

Even after a year studying in another country, without a vehicle, when Julie returns to her car at home, she can still drive it with the same degree of accuracy that she had before she went away. This is **retention** – the storing of discriminations and responses in long-term memory.

And when Julie goes to visit her parents, and borrows their much larger car to visit friends in her home town, she can drive with a very similar degree of accuracy because she has achieved **generalisation** of her driving skills to this new model of car.

What does fluency look like in reading? Learners begin with approximations which may frequently be inaccurate, making mistakes with sound-letter correspondences they have been exposed to, or being unsure what the link between letters and sounds might be. However, as they become more accurate, children decode the letters and sounds into whole words which (if they are in the child's spoken vocabulary) are understood. At this point the meaning of the text is becoming available to the child, but it would be a mistake to think that their reading skills are secure. We cannot be sure of this until the student has demonstrated fluency – that is, the decoding and subsequent recognition of words which takes place at a practically useful rate. Words which the child can read at fluency are much more likely to be retained in long-term memory, and can be recognised and used in different contexts because ready access to such memories frees up attention to concentrate on comprehension.

What this means is that fluency is a bottleneck. If a student only becomes accurate, and does not go on to develop fluency, long-term memory and generalisation are less stable and may fail completely for many items. This leaves the student struggling, despite the fact that, a few days previously, he or she may have read the same words with success. This pattern is repeated throughout education, across all subjects and activities. As a teacher, have you ever wondered why your students subsequently forgot something you had taught them? Assuming that your initial presentation of the information was clear, the most likely answer is that the students did not receive sufficient practice to fluency.

As far back as 1988, Carl Binder was able to assert, on the basis of thousands of empirical case studies of fluency:

> Many so-called learning disabilities turn out to be no more than a failure of the schools to measure and work towards fluency in basic skills … A few minutes per day of timed practice on carefully sequenced skills can often eliminate what were previously considered irremediable learning problems.[75]

The fact that schools have not yet addressed the fluency gap through providing sufficient 'carefully sequenced' practice is one of the major reasons for the gap between advantaged and disadvantaged students. Such practice is very efficient, uses little time, and costs almost nothing. Yet practice to high rates of fluency is rare in Western education.

Schools do, however, implicitly recognise this need when they seek to use programmes that increase reading 'mileage' and promote 'reading for pleasure'. The problem is that for the students who need the most help, the practice needs to be sequenced from a much earlier stage in their learning – at the letter-sound and word level. Once they have developed fluency in these prerequisite skills, reading becomes not only easier but more rewarding. It is not just the amount of practice but the careful sequencing of items and the rate of performance that are required for real progress in fluency.

So just how fast does a student need to read to be considered 'fluent' – that is, so that we can be confident of long-term retention, generalisation to new contexts, and working memory left over to attend to aspects of comprehension?[76] Binder, Haughton and Bateman provide estimates of a wide range of fluency criteria. For oral reading, fluent performance is 180–200 words per minute. For silent reading, therefore, we would expect an even higher rate. Consider part of an examination or test in which the student has a 600-word passage to read. For this section, the student must read the passage accurately, with understanding, and then be able to go back and answer specific questions about it, some of which will refer to explicit information and some to inferences or implications. The student will therefore need to read the whole passage at least twice, and probably more. It is not unreasonable to estimate that the student needs to read 1800 words in order to answer all the questions, and of course formulating the answers and recording them will take the bulk of the time. A student whose reading is laboured, halting or slow – even if it is accurate – will simply run out of time, or at best struggle to process all the information.

Binder, Haughton and Bateman sum up the educational impact of teaching without regard to fluency:

> Too often ... mastery to a given level of accuracy is the only goal. When that level is reached, or even before it is reached, the student is typically moved along immediately to new, more difficult material and never achieves fluency in the most basic skills. While the amount of work required and the level of expectation both increase, the student remains mired down, slowly and painfully logging along, falling further behind and becoming more discouraged.[76]

Does this sound like students you know? It is highly likely that what these students need is not special education programmes, but structured fluency practice in basic skills.

## Comprehension

Amongst all the disputes about reading, one thing is universally agreed: the goal of reading is comprehension. Too often, however, we have confused the goal with the means of achieving it. It is important to bear in mind that once the elements we have outlined above are securely in place, most reading comprehension problems will disappear, or improve a great deal.

That said, comprehension can neither be expected to develop on its own nor be taught in isolation from the many aspects of language and human culture that impinge upon our reading experience. It is not developed merely by administering comprehension tests (although repeated testing does tend to have a slight positive effect on learning). Ricketts, Sperring and Nation found that comprehension difficulties in mid to late childhood were linked to low educational attainment at 16 years, when students are making the important transition out of compulsory schooling into work, further education or training.[78] Such findings remind us that it is essential to ensure that all students are able to understand what they read, so that they can gain the knowledge they need to progress. In the next chapter we will consider how teachers can foster reading with comprehension in the regular classroom, even with struggling readers.

---

78  Ricketts, J., Sperring, R., & Nation, K. (2014). Educational attainment in poor comprehenders. *Frontiers in Psychology, 5*(Article 445), 1–11. Retrieved from www.frontiersin.org/articles/10.3389/fpsyg.2014.00445/full

# Chapter 4:
# Helping struggling readers
# in the secondary classroom

*Makele had come to London from Sierra Leone. He told me that his family decided to leave after the militia came house to house, searching for children to become child soldiers. His parents had saved their child by hiding him in a refrigerator. It had been a long road from there to his present life in London, and his early education had been patchy at best. He had had three years of education at my secondary school when I met him.*

*'He can't read or write,' his head of year explained at an English meeting.*

*'How do you mean?' asked a colleague. 'You don't mean...but why? How is that possible?'*

*'Don't know – he just can't.'*

*When I became Makele's teacher, his handwriting was literally a scrawl and neither he nor I could read it. But he was verbally fluent, lively and witty. I encouraged him to use a word processor so that we could work on his written language. To my surprise, he began to produce coherent sentences and I was now able to give him feedback. After this he made steady progress. He had clearly grasped the alphabetic principle, albeit frustratingly slowly at times.*

*There was no extra intervention available. So we talked a lot about the reading matter in class, and Makele began to take a constructive part in these discussions. It was as if he was just realising that he could understand as well as his peers. I set peer reading activities that gave him practice and small bursts of feedback on his reading. Gradually, we saw an improvement. He would read to me occasionally and there was always something to praise.*

*Above all, I told Makele and the rest of the class that with steady work, they would learn as well as anyone else. 'There is nothing wrong with you,' I would say regularly. 'You haven't learned to do this yet, but we're going to learn right now.' It was a message that was slow to sink in, but at the end of two years, Makele gained an exam pass two grades higher than he had been expected. It wasn't nearly enough for me, but it got him into higher education.*

*The point of this story is not to suggest that my teaching was extraordinary. On the contrary, I was an overstretched head of department in a challenging school. The things I did were neither extraordinary nor difficult. Any competent teacher could have done the same.*

*Except, in Makele's case, it appeared that they hadn't.*

There is often an expectation in secondary schools that if students haven't learned to read well by the time they begin Year 7, it's probably indicative of a lack of ability, or a disability. Actually, if we intervene effectively by changing the teaching, they can still become competent readers. In the meantime, what do we do about helping struggling readers to cope, and even improve, while grappling with the regular curriculum?

Hopefully by this point in the book you are well aware of the minefield that every day in school presents to the struggling adolescent reader. The fear of humiliation or embarrassment in front of one's peers is a constant spectre, as is teacher disapproval or feeling 'written off'. The demands in any lesson may lead to exposure, and frequently do. But the teacher's approach to managing reading problems in the classroom can make a major difference to a student's experience. We cannot expect any student to learn if they do not feel safe; we also need to have positive expectations of the student, which signal our confidence in their ability to learn. Here are some practical tips to making the classroom safer, and more successful, for struggling readers.

## 1. Know your students' reading skills, not just a general score

It might sound trivial, but it's not. School systems often fail to identify struggling readers. For example, Stothard, Snowling and Hulme found that only half the poor readers in their testing sample of 857 UK secondary school students had been identified as needing additional support.[79] Another trap for the teacher is that children can become experts at masking their reading problems in the classroom. They have plenty of motivation to do so, for to expose these problems is to invite shame, ridicule and bullying. So the careful teacher looks past the initial presentation and finds low-key ways to explore potential difficulties and see how deep they go. You can use more than test data for this: a quiet chat, a reading aloud exercise or a comprehension activity can also yield much information. But certainly, you should have a good idea of how your students stand in relation to national reading norms – regardless of your subject. If your school doesn't yet provide this data as standard to every teacher, the leadership may need a not-so-subtle nudge.

## 2. Have them read aloud to you

Library lessons are a great way to do this, as is simply taking the opportunity while moving around the room. Talking in a quiet voice (while keeping an eye on the rest of the class), invite the student to read a paragraph or more. As they read, note down the errors they make. Are they recurring, indicating a knowledge gap that can be taught, or are they inconsistent, suggesting inattention to details or a lack of fluency? Also, note how fluently and expressively they read. Most students love reading to their teacher, even those who

---

79 Stothard, S., Snowling, M., & Hulme, C. (2009). *The rate and identification of reading difficulties in secondary school pupils in England*. York: University of York; London: GL Assessment Limited.

are not confident about reading aloud to the class. Giving them an opportunity to read with you is a gift. Always remember to praise what they do well, and to give two or three very specific items of feedback. You can't do this sort of exercise all the time, but if you have two or three students like this with whom you check in every week, it makes a big difference to them. And, of course, it is likely that they will improve, because they are getting specific feedback and, hopefully, they want to please you.

## 3. Check their understanding

Some students seem to decode the words on the page quite well, but on probing a little deeper we may find that they have retained or understood very little. One reason for this may be a lack of fluency: decoding is so effortful that they have little working memory left over to process meaning. Another reason may be related to vocabulary; sometimes there are too many words on the page that they don't know, or aren't familiar with in this context. Asking them what a particular word means or asking them to rephrase a sentence can be very helpful in getting them to think more carefully. A critical element that enables students to understand texts is whether they are able to connect pronouns with their referents. Asking the student whom 'he' or 'it' refers to can reveal quite alarming gaps in their comprehension. So talk about language in a text with the class, and have specific students in mind to question most closely for understanding.

## 4. Pair them with an able buddy

This doesn't mean sitting them next to a clever pupil so that they can copy the answers. Set up activities where students read to each other in pairs. Get them to take turns, and tell them that they can work out between them which parts each will read, explaining that slower readers should read less text, focusing on accuracy. Even five or ten minutes of such activities will provide not only much-needed practice, but also modelling from an able peer. Modelling is most powerful when it is provided through someone who is close to the learner in age, status, and skill level. Students will generally take more risks with a peer than they would with an adult. Co-operative learning strategies (structured pair or group work, with clear ground rules to ensure productivity) have a strong track record in the research literature.[80]

## 5. Ground rules for a safe climate

It is essential to teach all students the ground rules for working co-operatively in this way:

- Don't tell your partner the word if they get stuck. Pause while they work it out.

- Read 'through' the word with them, don't just tell them the word, so that the learner can see the links between spellings and sounds.

- Always be polite when offering feedback. Never laugh or scold.

It may sound simple, but while being explicit about courtesy and respect never does harm, it often achieves much good.

## 6. Build up their spoken vocabulary

Reading represents spoken language. If students don't know the word on the page in their spoken vocabulary, they could have trouble decoding it, and even more so understanding the specific ways in which the term is being used. Using robust vocabulary instruction (as per Beck, McKeown and Kucan) will benefit all learners, but especially those furthest behind. Beck and her co-authors suggest that a student needs to encounter a word ten times in different contexts to make it likely that they will integrate it into their own vocabulary.[81] So intensify vocabulary instruction, and consciously plan which words to prioritise for study.

---

80 Johnson, R. T. & Johnson, D. W. (2002). *An overview of cooperative learning.* Retrieved from digsys.upc.es/ed/general/Gasteiz/docs_ac/Johnson_Overview_of_ Cooperative_Learning.pdf
81 Beck, I. L., McKeown, M. G., & Kucan, L. (2013). *Bringing words to life: robust vocabulary instruction.* New York, NY: The Guildford Press, p. 83

## 7. Vocabulary building in print

While building spoken vocabulary is important, remember that oral language alone cannot provide enough encounters with less frequent words to enable students to incorporate them into their vocabularies. For this, children need to read a lot, and this is why there is currently a strong movement to ensure that children are given challenging texts to read. The curriculum should lead students to the next step, not 'meet them where they are' and then leave them there. With students for whom encountering print and an enriched vocabulary is less likely – for instance, in economically disadvantaged homes – the teacher must ensure that there is a strand of explicit, systematic vocabulary instruction in all lessons. This one consideration has the potential to make a significant difference to outcomes for disadvantaged children because it is consciously addressing the cultural and language deficits that hold them back. Vocabulary not only enables us to be more articulate; it also widens our view of the world. For example, in order to understand the term 'Byzantine' as used in a news article about the arcane practices within government, the reader needs to have a sense of when and where the Byzantine Empire existed, and why it has become a byword for political machination.

## 8. Plan to include reading in all lessons

One of the key elements that is missing for poor readers in secondary school is practice. The difficulties in decoding and understanding text, and the motivational consequences of failing to extract meaning from text, mean that weak readers have strong incentives to avoid reading on a regular basis. Within the structure of the classroom, even short pieces of reading on a daily basis are useful. In addition to increasing the number of practice opportunities for the students, it is also useful to signal to them that reading is an essential and unavoidable part of daily life. On top of that, the rewards of gaining meaning from text over time tip the balance towards higher motivation. Lastly, frequency of contact with print can be an opportunity to desensitise the student to something that they have always feared.

It is not realistic to expect each classroom teacher to be able to design a reading-rich curriculum in their subject; this is a job for a team, with a clear lead from the faculty or department head. It can also be quite a mind shift for teachers who have limited reading activities in their lessons as they 'demotivate' students, or lead to outbreaks of disruptive behaviour.

This latter outcome, by the way, is an example of a dynamic where students manage teachers in order to reduce demands in lessons – disrupting the lesson, disengaging from the work, or becoming personally challenging. All of these are consequences that are unpleasant and aversive for teachers. If, by contrast, in a lesson with no reading demands the students are much more positive and pleasant, then it is easy to see how a strong (though often unconscious) motivation arises for the teacher to reduce reading or academic demands. This issue has to be addressed openly and explicitly with students: reading is a part of every lesson. Once students realise that this is non-negotiable, and that they are enjoying the benefits of wider knowledge and a broader vocabulary, success begins to create a 'virtuous circle'. But it may take a graduated process to establish such a system as part of the culture of the classroom.

## 9. Mix it up: low threat, high challenge

We shouldn't shy away from giving students tasks that they find challenging. The key thing is to do this in a climate that encourages honest attempts and is comfortable dealing with mistakes. By 'comfortable', we mean that it is understood that we will talk about why something was incorrect, so that the student learns what they needed to learn. In this sense, mistakes are the teacher's bread and butter. The emotional climate that we create around this is important. We should be relaxed, obviously without judgement, warm and firm. We can be consistent in pointing out errors and how to fix them because there is no embarrassment or humiliation involved. Teachers are sometimes schooled in their preparation courses to avoid anything that might demotivate a student, including pointing out an error. The semantic knots that we tie ourselves into as a result, where we try to prompt for a different answer without admitting that the student's first offering was wrong, are debilitating for a culture of authenticity and positive challenge. On the other hand, low-key, authentic praise goes a long way in building confidence, and this can be done as part of responding to a student's error. 'Good attempt. But remember that a reflection is not the same thing as a translation. I'll give you a minute to think about that and you can try again.'

One way of summing up this approach is the slogan 'low threat, high challenge'. For struggling readers, this means confidence that there will be opportunities for them to try things that they might fail at, that they will get reliable corrective feedback, that this will be low key, and that, even in the case of errors, their status with the teacher will be undiminished.

## 10. Hierarchies of skills

We looked earlier at the Stages of Learning. It is possible to teach the same knowledge or skill in different dimensions: for example, at acquisition, at accuracy, and at fluency. It is essential for the teacher to recognise that while some students may be at fluency, and others 'only' accurate, there may be others who are reading at the acquisition stage. Remember that just because a student has become accurate, that does not mean we can be sure that the learning will endure. To be sure of this, we need to provide practice to fluency. We can do this with short bursts of prose reading, reading lists of subject-specific keywords, and retrieval practice. However, students working at the acquisition level will need closely monitored practice, with immediate correction of errors so that these do not become ingrained habits.

## 11. Repeated quizzing

One way of building students' confidence and self-esteem is to ensure that every lesson starts with a review of previous learning. This regular retrieval of key knowledge helps the student to store it in long-term memory and, combined with the practice effect of testing, creates the opportunity to have students begin each lesson with a very high proportion of correct answers. Such success builds motivation and sets them up with a positive view of what can be achieved.

Repeated quiz questions do not have to be the same every time. For example, the following three questions all require the same knowledge from a student of geography:

- What is the longest river in China?
- What is the third longest river in the world?
- On what river is the Chinese city of Shanghai?

In this way, the quizzes repeat the testing of knowledge without being repetitive.

Such quizzes may have a direct or indirect relationship to reading, depending on whether students have access to text; what is important, though, is that over time the student begins to perceive him or herself as capable of learning because the repeated exposure helps them to remember. This feeds into their willingness to understand (and remember) the content of written texts. Whether the student is a capable reader or not, the growth in confidence and self-esteem from such a regime builds motivation.

## 12. Include regular (daily) spelling practice in your routines

Spelling is the flip side of the coin to reading. When students spell they are using the written code in the opposite direction to reading, but the correspondences between sounds and spellings remain unchanged. Spelling, therefore, strengthens reading, and *vice versa*.

There are three main approaches to spelling: whole word, phonic and morphological.

- The **whole word** approach asks students to memorise a word as a whole. Sometimes teachers resort to this as some very frequent words have unusual spellings – that is, they rarely occur in other words. However, this method has severe limitations and can suggest to students that the relationships between sounds and spellings in English are random and cannot be relied upon (which is incorrect).

- **Phonic** spelling teaches students the relationships between spellings and sounds. The student orally segments the word and writes a grapheme for each phoneme, finally blending what they have written to check for accuracy. For multisyllabic words, train students to break each word into syllables before spelling each phoneme, *eg* 'de-ci-pher'. Doing this explicitly and systematically is very important to ensure that all students acquire the body of knowledge that they need to master the written code.

- **Morphological** spelling teaches students to recognise and spell words in parts, through units of meaning (morphemes). The theory is that combinations of these morphemes will greatly enhance the student's vocabulary as well as provide opportunities to master spelling.

Spelling practice can take just a few minutes a day. Students work in pairs, test one another from each student's personalised lists, and provide corrective feedback. A cumulative bar graph is a good way to record how many new words each student is able to spell. For a description of an effective classroom approach to spelling using student self-correction, see Heron, Okyere and Miller.[82]

## 13. Add systematic language teaching including syntax, morphology and etymology

Another strategy which only requires limited lesson time but which has important cumulative effects is that of word study. By this we mean the explicit, systematic teaching of how words work. There are three main areas to explore: syntax, morphology, and etymology.

- **Syntax** is 'the study of grammatical relations between words and other units within the sentence'.[83] It includes the way that words

82  Heron, T. E., Okyere, B. A., & Miller, A. D. (1991). A Taxonomy of Approaches to Teach Spelling. *Journal of Behavioral Education, 1*(1), 117–130. Retrieved from link. springer.com/article/10.1007/BF00956757

83  Matthews, P. H. (2014). *The concise Oxford dictionary of linguistics.* Oxford: OUP

can be changed to suit meaning, and how changes in verb endings (inflections) or word order can change meaning. For example, it can be important for some learners to be explicitly shown the ways in which verbs change their endings using '-s' or '-es', '-ing', or '-ed' – even if English is their first language. For example, in science, the term 'hypothesis' can be expanded by a brief discussion where the word becomes a verb (hypothesise) and is then used in several contexts: 'Galileo tested his hypothesis at the Tower of Pisa'; 'Galileo hypothesised that objects would fall towards earth at the same rate regardless of weight'; 'hypothesising is an essential part of experimental design'.

Likewise, the ways in which tenses are formed in English is much more important to meaning than native speakers may realise: what is the difference in meaning, for example, between 'I was going to the lake', 'I went to the lake' and 'I used to go to the lake'? Highlighting and explaining potentially confusing or subtle syntax is important to promoting students' understanding.

- **Morphology** is the way in which parts of words carry meaning, and how changes to these parts (morphemes) change the meaning. Obvious morphemes are prefixes ('un-', 'im-', 'trans-', 'para-', *etc*) and suffixes ('-ment', '-ism', '-ation', *etc*). Identifying suffixes and prefixes enables learners to then identify the root word, for example 'govern' in 'government' or 'fide' in 'confide' and 'confidence'. Learning to identify (and spell) these morphemes is very liberating for students who had not previously realised that there are distinct patterns in the ways that words are arranged, combined and modified in English.

- **Etymology** is the study of a word's history. We often don't realise the long and varied journey of a word to its place in our everyday language. Unpacking this history can greatly enrich our understanding of our own language. Consider the word 'nice', which these days is a bland, superficial word generally meaning pleasant or kind. Several hundred years ago it meant specific, fastidious, or scrupulous, so that Hamlet, for example, accuses himself of 'thinking too nicely upon the point', instead of taking action. Awareness of changes in word meaning is essential to exploring older English literature, as most secondary school exam syllabi require. But etymology can also enrich subjects like science and mathematics as it opens opportunities to link the knowledge of the lesson with stories and thence to culture and history. For example, the term 'isosceles', describing a triangle with exactly two sides of equal length, is based on the Greek words '*isos*' (meaning equal) and '*skelos*' (meaning leg). Repeated exposure to short explanations of word origins and historical uses helps students to make more subtle lexical distinctions – to recognise the shades of meaning in words, and the specific ways in which they can and cannot be used.

## 14. Building comprehension

In addition to knowledge of vocabulary, morphology, syntax, and accuracy of decoding, comprehension is also built via the domains of background knowledge, identifying and distinguishing main ideas, inference and reasoning skills.

- **Background knowledge**

   Daniel Willingham argues that teaching specific comprehension strategies is useful and can have impact. However, these gains can be achieved in a relatively short time and thereafter, extended training in comprehension strategies does not lead to additional gains. Instead, Willingham argues that schools could invest time more profitably if they also build students' background knowledge.[84]

   Such knowledge is essential for drawing logical conclusions and picking up inferences. If a student doesn't know that Venus is a very hot planet, she is not going to pick up on the implied meanings in an advertising slogan such as 'hotter than Mercury, cooler than Venus'. Further, if she doesn't know that Venus is

---

84 Willingham, D. T. (Winter 2006/07). Ask the cognitive scientist: the usefulness of brief instruction in reading comprehension strategies. *American Educator, 30*(4), 39–45, 50.

the seductive goddess of love, she won't pick up on the play of words between science and mythology. She might even form a misconception, gaining the mistaken impression that Venus is a cool planet while Mercury is hot. In fact, they are both very hot.

- **Main idea**

   A key goal of comprehension instruction is to enable students to identify 'the main idea', and more specifically to identify superordinate and subordinate ideas. In other words, which one is the bigger idea, or which idea is more important in a particular text? Bob Dixon and colleagues developed a useful strategy for this based on the idea of identifying all the referents to a previously stated topic or idea in a passage. This resulted in a Direct Instruction programme for reading comprehension called *SRA Reading Success* which develops this, and related principles, over a series of lessons. Perhaps the simplest way to employ this strategy is to check that students are correctly linking pronouns to the original nouns. It is surprising how often students are unclear on who 'she' or 'they' might have been in a passage. Clearing up these confusions is straightforward and immediately enables students to access what may previously have been baffling text.

- **Inference**

   There are three kinds of inferences that we may draw from a text: logical inferences, probable inferences and possible inferences.

   *Logical inferences* are those which must be true, even though they are not stated, because of other statements. If Amy invited five friends to go camping, and only two didn't come, how many people went camping? (Four – three friends plus Amy.) If a character arrived home at seven o'clock, they must have been elsewhere before that. And so on.

   *Probable inferences* are likely to be drawn from a text and from our personal knowledge. If the passage says that 'Ahmed ate four sandwiches when he got home from school', a probable inference is that he was hungry. There are of course other *possible inferences*, *eg* that Ahmed had not had lunch, or that he was greedy. Fiction writers frequently invite readers to speculate in order to generate possible inferences. This keeps the reader's imagination actively engaged, and adds to suspense and narrative power. For example, in 'The tall man stood at the door for some time before he finally knocked', the writer doesn't tell us why the man paused, or even who he is, but we know that this detail must be important, so we begin to speculate: he is hesitant; he has doubts about his course of action; he is waiting for something or someone; he is listening. It is not important that the speculations should be correct at this stage – these will be confirmed or otherwise as the story proceeds. What is important is that we have considered the possibilities. Students need to be conscious that such opportunities are deliberately contrived by authors to help draw their attention to important ideas. Practice with inferences can happen both incidentally, as the teacher works through a text with students, or more systematically, for example as starter activities.

- **Reasoning**

  Precise use of logic and reasoning is also an essential part of developing reading comprehension. This is particularly important as we seek to develop independent critical thought. There are very few programmes that set out to teach students important logical patterns, like analogies, or logical fallacies (*Corrective Reading Comprehension* is one that does). Once students get used to spotting anomalies, they may even find the exercise fun. For example, at a simple level, we can ask students to explain what is wrong with this syllogism:

  - All Dalmatians have spots.
  - My cat has spots.
  - Therefore my cat is a Dalmatian.

  Common logical fallacies include *ad hominem*, straw man, argument from authority, false cause and middle ground. Teaching students to identify logical fallacies arms them with powerful tools and also, hopefully, helps them to avoid such mistakes themselves.

In summary, reading comprehension can be taught through developing students' reasoning, inference and deduction skills, and is also built by strengthening background knowledge, vocabulary, language skills and memory training. Some specific strategy training is desirable; but explicit teaching of knowledge is also vital for strong comprehension.

## 15. Communicate positive expectations

Lastly, going back to the opening point of this chapter: if we communicate to students that they can learn, they will. If we communicate to them that they will never learn, they will give up. And then they will do something else (which usually involves making the teacher's life more difficult!). So, while using strategies like those above are helping the struggling reader, they are also making a difference for the teacher and other students in the class. It is in everyone's interest when all students are making progress in their reading – there are no losers.

# Chapter 5:
# What school leaders need to know and do about reading

*'We have a group of students who aren't making the progress that they should. They're mostly willing to learn, but they're being held back by low literacy. What can we do?'*

*It wasn't the first time I'd had this conversation, and I knew it wouldn't be the last. All over the world, our education systems have reproduced the phenomenon of a group of students who are reading far below the level that they need to succeed at secondary school.*

*'What information do you have about the cohort's literacy profiles?' I asked.*

*'Well, we have their reading scores from when they arrived two years ago, and some of the SEN students have more recent assessment information. Basically, the students we're concerned about have reading ages three to seven years behind where they need to be.'*

*I left aside the question of how much weight could be given to two-year-old data, and how the school had identified the 'students of concern'. 'Are you finding that this group is having an impact in the classroom in terms of disruption and poor behaviour?'*

*'Oh, yes. Their teachers are very frustrated and concerned.'*

*Shifting perspective, I asked, 'What has been your whole-school strategy so far for dealing with the problem of low reading?'*

*'Hmmm. I guess we're looking for a good intervention to get their reading scores up.'*

*'How about we take a look at your screening systems, and then at what happens in the classroom? You might find that many of the problems can be addressed without any extra interventions.'*

The focus of this chapter is on how school leaders can manage the culture as well as the systems of their community to enhance progress in reading, especially for those who have encountered difficulties in the past. That includes change not only in how interventions operate, but also how we do business daily in our classrooms.

## Behaviour

It should go without saying, but underlying all our efforts is the need to establish safety and high standards of behaviour. It is only within such a climate that teaching and learning can take place. While it is outside the scope of this book to explore the 'how' and 'why' of good behaviour, it is worth stating explicitly that any attempt to tackle curriculum and literacy demands without first establishing safe conditions for learning is doomed to fail.

A second reason for consciously attending to behaviour first is that strong systems will collect data to reveal patterns that can then be addressed intentionally. An obvious example is where a teacher is having ongoing difficulties with a class or individuals: we can put in appropriate support, such as an extra pair of eyes to observe students, to give feedback to the teacher, and to help them collect the data they need to review their practice. A perhaps less obvious way in which information on behaviour can be revealing is through checking the correlation between students' reading scores and the frequency of their appearance in the school's data on behaviour problems. In one school we worked with, a senior leader found that there was an almost direct correspondence between how far behind students were in their reading and how poorly they scored in the behaviour points system. Such observations are not possible if good data is not collected.

Some will no doubt resist the notion that poor reading is a direct cause of misbehaviour. As with so many aspects of human behaviour, there are of course a range of student responses to persistent reading difficulties:

> A few studies have evaluated whether poor reading performance negatively impacts 'distal' feelings and behaviours that are not specific to reading activities. In these studies, poor readers have been reported to be more likely to act out or be aggressive (*eg*, Morgan, Farkas, & Wu, 2009; Trzesniewski, Moffitt, Caspi, Taylor, & Maughan, 2006), distractible and inattentive (Goldston *et al*, 2007; Morgan, Farkas, Tufis, & Sperling, 2008), and anxious and depressed (Arnold *et al*, 2005; Carroll, Maughan, Goodman, & Meltzer, 2005). Older poor readers have been reported to be more likely to consider or attempt suicide (Daniel *et al*, 2006). … Morgan, Farkas, and Qiong (2012) report that their analyses 'indicated that poor readers are at substantially greater risk of socioemotional maladjustment. This was the case across multiple self-report measures as well as after extensive statistical control of possible confounding factors.'[85]

Any school leader overseeing behaviour and safety must ensure that part of the plan for improving students' conduct (and indeed, their experience of school) is to ensure that they can read properly. If there is just one message in this book that we want to communicate, it is that nearly every student can be taught to read. If we neglect this fundamental responsibility, we should also take responsibility for the consequent effects on student behaviour and mental health. If the means for solving the reading problem are within our grasp, we have a moral obligation

---

85  Hempenstall, K. (2013, November. Updated 2016). Literacy and behaviour. Retrieved from www.nifdi.org/resources/news/hempenstall-blog/405-literacy-and-behaviour

to apply them. We would suggest that it is doubly wrong to fail to do so, then let the students carry the consequences.

## Good quality data on student reading

The second key principle is that schools need to have accurate, up-to-date data on the essential basic skills that are required to access the curriculum across the range of subjects. In practice, this means reading, spelling, writing skills, and mathematics essentials such as number concepts, place value and times tables. Many schools establish a baseline using standardised tests in reading and mathematics when students first arrive, but this information is most often used to rank students and then allocate them to 'sets' or 'tracks'. It is important to note that standardised test results are rarely expressed in a way that is helpful for identifying specific teaching needs; and indeed, this is not really their function. They are designed to enable us to compare a student's performance with the wider population. Beyond that, we need to have much more precise, curriculum-linked measures that will give us a baseline from which to identify students in need of help, and then to target help at the gaps in their current knowledge or skill levels.

An example is the use of a simple ten-minute writing sample, administered under standard but easily replicable conditions. One way of doing this is for each English teacher to make this one of the first activities of the school year. Introducing herself, she can tell the students that they are going to introduce themselves to her by writing a letter. The teacher brainstorms with the students all the different topics they could write about to describe themselves – family, friends, their neighbourhood, pets, hobbies, sports, books, films, food, and so on. The teacher then issues lined paper, and tells students that for this exercise they are going to take just ten minutes. 'I will tell you when you have two minutes and one minute left. Don't worry about correcting any spelling or punctuation errors – I will give you an extra two minutes once we stop writing to check your work and make any corrections that are needed.' The teacher takes questions and checks with individual students to ensure they are clear on the task, then times the group for ten minutes, with time announcements at eight and nine minutes. The teacher gives students two minutes to identify any errors by circling them (not erasing them), and correcting as many as they have time for. Finally, the teacher asks students to count the number of words they wrote and to write this number at the lower right of the page, with a circle around the number.

Although this is a simple procedure, it has many advantages. First, it is contextual. Students have a pragmatic reason for engaging, *ie* they are indeed introducing themselves to the teacher. Secondly, they have also contributed to the ideas for writing and have already been primed for the exercise. This ensures that there is no 'artificial ceiling' effect where students do not show their writing ability because they were stuck for ideas. Thirdly, the conditions are standardised, which means that the work students produce across the cohort is comparable. Further, the teacher now has a great deal of baseline information about students' spelling, punctuation, grammar, vocabulary, handwriting and writing speed.

The most immediate tasks for using this baseline data are:

- to identify those who produced limited and/or poor quality work.
- to collate these results in order to prioritise those students who need help most urgently.
- to identify the areas of writing skills in which students will need support.

These findings will then affect the way that support resources are allocated. Without this data, the only other recourse the school has is either to a standardised testing regime, which is far too imprecise, or to a referral system in which the teachers who push hardest get extra resources for their students. It is an unfortunate truth that such advocacy is not always as altruistic as we might like – in some teachers' minds, referring students for 'SEN support' can be a way of offloading responsibility for them. It is far better to have hard data that we can use to inform our teaching.

## Use a multi-tiered screening system

There are two major traps that schools can fall into with reading intervention: not providing for students who need help, and misdirecting intervention support at students who do not really need it. When it comes to working out which students we should give extra help, and what sort of help they need, one or even two tests will not be enough. We recommend a screening system with a minimum of three tiers:

**Tier 1**

A regular standardised test with a strong statistical base, whose underlying model of reading includes both phonological decoding and comprehension.

**Tier 2**

For those who are found to be reading at or below the 35th percentile compared to the national population, run a second standardised test. This is to check for two issues – namely, measurement error and motivation. All standardised tests have a built-in 'standard error' of measurement, which is the statistical probability that on another occasion, or with a different set of test items, the student might score higher or lower. This second test is an opportunity to identify 'outliers' who may score low on a first testing occasion, but are actually stronger readers than this result indicated. The other reason for this second test is to see whether low motivation played a part in the low scores of some students. It is not uncommon to see large variations between tests because, on the first occasion, the student was not trying their hardest. Experience shows that up to half of the lowest scorers (*ie* those scoring in the bottom third of the population) can improve their score enough to move out of this category simply by sitting a second standardised test. We have seen some students increase their scores by four years between two standardised tests, sat only weeks apart.

**Tier 3**

This tier is for those who still fell into the bottom third of the national percentile ranking after two standardised tests. Use a one-to-one, detailed assessment which involves reading carefully graded prose, to determine:

- the extent of gaps in decoding knowledge.

- poor reading habits that lead to careless errors.

- motivational factors.

- comprehension issues.

To implement this tier will require training of staff to a high degree of fluency in such assessment, so that they are able to consistently identify all the students' reading errors, and to interpret them accurately.

Using such a multi-tiered system enables us to identify and target those students who are most in need, and to provide appropriate support for others without the difficulty and expense of more intensive interventions when these are not indicated. For school leaders, decisions to allocate limited resources must be based on thorough, detailed assessment information. A failure to invest time and resources at this point of the process can lead to considerable unnecessary expense – and ineffective practice – later on.

## Applying the data to resourcing decisions

Once we have established the types of reading difficulties students have, we can set about allocating staffing and resources accordingly. For example, students who are only a short way behind may benefit from a paired reading intervention where they read to an adult who also models good reading. Such adults, with training, can provide specific feedback on student reading errors, and ask questions to elicit deeper comprehension. There are also structured decoding programmes which work well for students reading up to two years behind. For students reading further behind, staff will need a higher level of training for a more intensive intervention (see Chapter 6). For students who are decoding well, but have a high rate of comprehension errors, the school can put in place a comprehension-focused intervention which can be delivered in small groups.

School leaders are only in a position to allocate these resources once they have accurate assessment information about the different levels and types of needs that the tiered screening system has revealed.

## Policy and Curriculum

In order to deliver interventions to those who need them, school leaders need to ensure that there is a clearly developed policy around reading and the curriculum. Given that reading is critical to accessing the curriculum at secondary school, for life chances, and for social engagement and self-esteem, we argue that such a policy statement would include the following provisions:

**Development of reading skills will be given a high priority in every subject.**

This helps to ensure that students are equipped to acquire subject-specific knowledge, to develop a wide academic vocabulary, to encounter a range of text types and to practise their reading fluency by greatly increasing the number of words they encounter in any given week.

**Students may be withdrawn from any subject for effective reading intervention.**

If every subject benefits from improved reading, and if reading is a whole-school priority, then it makes sense for every subject to contribute a little of the catch-up time some students need. The condition, of course, is that the positive impact of the intervention far outweighs the negative impact of withdrawal from classes. (See Chapter 6 for what constitutes a 'high-impact' reading intervention.)

**All students at risk of reading failure will be identified and helped.**

This is where the school commits to a thorough, systematic screening process like the one described above, so that no student is missed. Many schools still rely on teacher identification when allocating support, and this is fraught with error, particularly because many poor readers have developed sophisticated ways of masking their reading problems – for example, disruptive behaviour, playing the class clown, fading into the background, or absenteeism. Thorough, objective screening, followed by prompt and decisive action, is required to ensure that all students are picked up and helped.

**No student will leave school unable to read at their age level.**

This implies a school commitment to ensure that students get the help that they need, and that this help has been rigorously evaluated to ensure that it is effective. Interventions which will enable complete catch-up do exist, but implementing them requires a high level of training and a strong commitment to fidelity of delivery. This policy provision is a test of the leadership team's ability to communicate vision and mission, as well as their organisational skills.

## Develop a corpus of effective teaching strategies which are used across all subject areas

The previous chapter describes a range of appropriate strategies which are of benefit to students with poor reading at secondary school. These include explicit vocabulary instruction, explicit and systematic language teaching, acquisition of background (contextual) knowledge, reasoning skills and inference skills. Such strategies are appropriate in many different domains and contexts. (See Chapter 4 for examples of how these approaches can be applied.)

It should also be said that these strategies will be of benefit to *all* students. We recommend *Reading Reconsidered* by Lemov, Driggs and Woolway[86] and *Bringing Words to Life* by Beck, McKeown and Kucan[87] for insightful, practical strategies on how to ensure that the classroom provides the depth of instruction needed to acquire greater competency in reading skills.

In the past, school curricula have sometimes been under pressure to reduce demands on students because they did not have the necessary cultural knowledge to deal with more sophisticated or challenging texts. The cumulative effect of this process was to disadvantage those who were already disadvantaged by a lack of relevant knowledge. Instead, school curricula can compensate for such a lack of knowledge by ensuring that students are appropriately supported to access more demanding texts.

---

86  Lemov, D., Driggs, C., & Woolway, E. (2016). *Reading reconsidered: a practical guide to rigorous literacy instruction.* San Francisco, CA: Jossey-Bass.
87  Beck, I. L., McKeown, M. G., & Kucan, L. (2013). *Bringing words to life.*

This is why the teaching approaches mentioned above are so important: they all provide the extra scaffolding that is required for students to reach a greater depth of understanding – even for those students who are the prime concern of this book, the 20% who arrive at secondary school reading well behind their peers. Relying on intervention alone for these students will not equip them with the knowledge or experience they need – rather, effective intervention will give them the tools that they need to participate in wider classroom discourse and activity. It is therefore essential to ensure that the quality of their classroom experience will support and challenge them.

It should not be assumed that teachers already have the skills necessary to undertake these challenges. The process of embedding these strategies into the curricula of different subjects, and of developing the skills required to a practical level of fluency, may take several years to permeate an entire school community. School leaders will need to introduce initiatives in stages, with peer-to-peer development activities and regular review points to reflect on workload, staff perceptions and impact on student achievement. Part of being professional involves developing the skills to interpret and judiciously apply educational research, and this topic should be high on the agenda in every secondary school's professional development programme.

## Set school culture to make classrooms emotionally safe for those struggling with reading

This is not about developing an emotionally driven or work-avoidant culture, but one where teachers are sensitive to student needs and are able to work with these students over time to build their confidence through a series of small successes as they face achievable challenges. Like the process of strengthening knowledge in the curriculum described above, such a climate is developed and embedded in a school's culture over time. For example, a professional development programme could include training on how to ask 'concept check' questions, where students are presented with two alternative interpretations, but only one is logically viable. Such questions act as prompts and also as checks of student understanding for the teacher. Other examples could include: how to give accurate and constructive feedback when students make errors reading aloud; how to teach vocabulary through additive instruction; and how to provide corrective feedback on logical errors.

Senior leaders on their own cannot make school culture change overnight. Recruiting middle leaders to your cause – and ensuring a depth of understanding amongst this team – is essential. These leaders in turn will nurture their teams, highlighting and sharing good practice wherever they find it, both formally and informally. For example, it may be appropriate to discuss a resource, activity or questioning technique in the more formal setting of a departmental meeting; alternatively, it may be equally effective to encourage a colleague informally to help build the positive culture that you seek. As Nick Rose has pointed out, sometimes subtle tweaks are much more powerful than full-on 'interventions' in shifting mindset.[88]

There is a flip side which is at least equally challenging. This is the tendency in some school cultures to disparage those who struggle most with their reading. There are deeply ingrained beliefs (and prejudices) in schools, as in wider society, about the nature of intelligence, and the relative value of students considered to have different levels of intelligence. While it may be common to human nature to pigeonhole others, and to determine social hierarchies based on attributes such as beauty, intelligence, wealth, or even patriotism, as teachers we have to actively resist such tendencies. If we do not, we cannot hope to challenge the injustices of education systems where 20% of students are effectively earmarked for failure. Senior leaders can model optimistic, ambitious attitudes for students, and to challenge – as constructively as possible – narratives or allusions which imply that some students are without hope. Often such comments are not meant unkindly; but tolerating such beliefs within a school culture lowers teacher expectations and ultimately undermines progress for these students.

It can be particularly difficult when older or more senior colleagues are in the habit of such throwaway lines. 'I saw Brian today,' the head says. 'He

---

88  Rose, N. J. (2014). Growth mindset: it's not magic. Retrieved from evidenceintopractice. wordpress.com/2014/06/01/growth-mindset-its-not-magic/

seemed quite lost. I can't even see him getting a job in a burger bar.' The head shakes his head pityingly, but the message to anyone within earshot is: the head thinks that there's no achievement possible for Brian – and by extrapolation, for other students whom they think of as 'like Brian'.

Here are three simple ways to make school culture more supportive of students with reading difficulties:

1. Provide staff with repeated anecdotes of achievement for 'low attainers'. For example, we encourage leaders to routinely share intervention data demonstrating significant improvement. Such improvements, often unexpected by mainstream teachers, alert them to previously unsuspected potential and open up the possibility of greater levels of challenge.

2. Have mature conversations with students who are not considered 'able' – conversations which imply that you perceive intelligence and ability. Ask them about their interests and achievements, comment on something positive you have heard about them, and ask them questions about their subjects, exam preparation or future plans. This kind of respectful attention is a powerful influence on young people's self-esteem and can, over time, greatly improve their sense of engagement in school. Couple it with effective intervention and you have a winning combination.

3. Raise staff awareness of the ways in which poor reading makes students more vulnerable to bullying. Make staff conscious of apparently minor classroom interactions which can be very painful for students, and use this to underpin professional development around 'safe classrooms' where ridicule, teasing or put-downs are never acceptable. Having zero tolerance for bullying includes zero tolerance for the kinds of comments and humiliation that struggling readers often face.

## Don't expect more from reading promotion schemes than they can deliver

All too often we see reading promotion schemes being labelled as 'literacy interventions'. In the broadest sense of the term, if the school uses a software package that is intended to increase the amount of reading that students do, it has intervened. But if the programme applies to all students, the term 'intervention' does not seem appropriate, since 'intervention' would seem to suggest that an action is targeted at a particular group. This is not mere semantics: some schools rely on such schemes as the mainstay of their support for struggling readers. A placement test identifies which students have difficulty with reading; a range of easier-to-read books is indicated, and the student is expected to read these books. A study of one such scheme by the Education Endowment Foundation (2015) found that the weakest readers could not access the programme's books independently.[89] While a reading promotion scheme may work to encourage the amount of reading students do, it is not designed to do anything to close the gaps that students may have from a chequered learning history. This is a job for trained teachers, armed with a well-designed programme. School leaders need to be very clear about who is expected to benefit from these very different initiatives. In short, if you are using a reading promotion scheme in the belief that it will help your weakest readers learn to read, you are likely to be disappointed.

## Beware labelling cultures and work to eliminate them

One of the most insidious ways in which schools limit educational achievement is through the dispensation of labels to explain why a child has not learned. Traditionally, teachers and schools have found a wide variety of options to explain away learning problems. For example, in a US study of 5000 students evaluated by school psychologists to determine why they were doing poorly in class, 'All 5000 evaluations attributed the student's problems to deficiencies *in the child* and the child's family. *Not one* linked the student's problems to faulty curricula, poor teaching practices or bad management.'[90]

89 Gorard, S., Siddiqui, N., & See, B. H. (2015). *Accelerated Reader.* Education Endowment Foundation and Durham University. Retrieved from v1.educationendowmentfoundation.org.uk/uploads/pdf/Accelerated_Reader_(Final). pdf

90 Barbash, S. (2012). *Clear teaching: with Direct Instruction, Siegfried Engelmann discovered a better way of teaching.* Education Consumers Foundation. Retrieved from education-consumers.org/pdf/CT_111811.pdf

By way of illustration, let's take the case of Kevin. Kevin is based on many students we have worked with. After a slow start with reading, his teacher concludes that he does not have enough exposure to print at home and asks his mother to read with him more. The family is seen as the source of the problem. Two years later, and with very little progress, Kevin's teacher interprets this as a developmental problem – he will read 'when he's ready', she says. Later in his schooling, as his motivation declines and he finds class boring and frustrating, Kevin is assessed and found to have 'moderate learning difficulties'.

By the time he reaches secondary school Kevin is labelled as SEN, with moderate learning difficulties and emotional/mental health needs including possible ADHD. The special needs coordinator allocates him to a literacy intervention and the teacher explains to Kevin that he has dyslexia, dyspraxia, and a hyperactivity disorder. This means that Kevin is always going to have difficulty with learning but that the school will give him every support to cope with his education.

Kevin now has a number of clear messages:

- The problems he has had with reading and other schoolwork are caused by something that is wrong with him.
- There is nothing anyone can do to fix this.
- There is no hope of real success; his time at school is now to be endured rather than enjoyed.

What this process has achieved is not progress for Kevin, but the provision of labels to paper over the fact that his teachers lacked the necessary skills to teach Kevin to read. The assumption was that if other students learned to read, the teacher must be doing the right thing, and therefore there is something wrong with Kevin.

There is, however, another interpretation. Perhaps these students learned to read because, as Louisa Moats points out, most students will learn to read successfully regardless of the method used to teach them, while others will only learn to read if provided with explicit systematic instruction.[91]

---

91 Moats, L. C. (1999). *Teaching reading is rocket science.* [PDF version]. American Federation of Teachers. Retrieved from www.aft.org/sites/default/files/reading_rocketscience_2004.pdf.

In this case, Kevin's lack of progress needs to be re-examined. Was his failure inevitable? Almost certainly not.

Explaining possible causes of reading failure, Vellutino *et al*[92] point out:

Clay (1987) [contends] that reading difficulties in beginning readers are, in most cases, caused primarily by experiential and/ or instructional deficits. Indeed, the impaired reader sample initially identified in first grade, using exclusionary criteria such as those typically used to identify disabled readers in such research, represented approximately 9% of the (available) population from which these children were drawn. Yet, the impaired readers who continued to qualify for this diagnosis after only one semester of remediation represented only 1.5% of the population from which these children were drawn, which is a far cry from the 10% to 15% figures that have emerged as estimates of the incidence of reading disability in the relevant literature.

In other words, reading difficulties were overcome in 85% of students fitting a dyslexic profile in just one semester – simply through effective teaching.

The implications of such findings are sobering. How many students are reaching secondary school with poor reading, not because they have a disability but because they did not get access to high-quality, explicit instruction at an early enough stage? Even at secondary school, it is still not too late. For example, one review of interventions for adolescent reading found that:

A compelling evidence base has developed for intervening with adolescent struggling readers (Biancarosa and Snow, 2006; Kamil *et al*, 2008). Multiple small-scale, investigator-led studies document strategies for improving older students' reading ability, and recent syntheses of this research base, including several meta-analyses

92  Vellutino, F. R., Fletcher, J. M., Snowling, M.J., & Scanlon, D. M. (2004). Specific reading disability (dyslexia): what have we learned in the past four decades? *Journal of Child Psychology and Psychiatry*, 45(1), 2–40.

(Edmonds *et al*, 2009; Scammacca *et al*, 2007), have reported mean treatment effects in the moderate-sized range.[93]

School leaders must be careful not to accept a version of support that consists of simply assigning labels and then allowing these labels to explain a lack of progress. Such practices are discriminatory, and work to disadvantage students through lowered expectations, while increasing their sense of frustration through a growing sense of powerlessness.

## Adhere to transparent, rigorous evaluation processes

In addition to challenging cultures of labelling and low expectations, school leaders need to ensure that the support which has been provided to students is having the intended impact. Very often the responsibility for targeted help is allocated to the Special Education/Inclusion/Support department – but with little active oversight.

There are a number of reasons why this happens. Obviously some managers are stretched for time, and trust or hope that the SEN team has everything under control.

Another reason is that school leaders without a background in special education can find it difficult to question statements which are full of unfamiliar, professional-sounding jargon: 'Estrella has dyspraxia and her profile indicates that an auditory processing disorder may be complicating her ability to respond to instructions, so she finds school very difficult, even with the coloured paper we've provided to help with her Irlen syndrome'. In reality, what has been offered here is three hypothesised (and largely unverifiable) reasons why Estrella is not making progress. The first question for the school leader to ask is: 'What practical strategies will you use to help Estrella make progress?'; along with a follow-up question: 'How will you know whether what you are doing is working?'. These questions are reasonable, responsible and focused on how we will help Estrella rather than why we can't help her. No one should be paid a teaching salary to explain why a child can't be helped.

---

93  Vaughn, S. & Fletcher, J. M. (2012). Response to intervention with secondary school students with reading difficulties. *Journal of Learning Disabilities, 45*(3), 244–256. Retrieved from www.ncbi.nlm.nih.gov/pmc/articles/PMC3356920/

A third reason that senior leaders do not always monitor progress closely for those receiving intervention is the unconscious expectation that such students are lacking in potential, and the best we can expect is for them to be nurtured until such time as they move on. It is worth noting that effective interventions can dramatically affect progress, and therefore low-achieving students should be seen as an opportunity for the school to add significant value to student outcomes. Professor Greg Brooks points out that for literacy interventions, 'Good impact – sufficient to at least double the standard rate of progress – can be achieved, and it is reasonable to expect it'.[94]

There are two ways in which school leaders can monitor progress. The first is the global view, where the progress of the group is reported using pre- and post-test measures. For example, a phonics intervention might be run for four months. In that time, the mean reading age of students moves from 9.5 to 11.2. This averaged approach is a traditional way of summarising the impact of an intervention. On the face of it, this result is good news. However, as anyone who has collated such data knows, an approach like this can be used to paper over many problems. The result could be distorted by outliers at either end. Most students may have made less progress than the average, but a few made a lot more. Conversely, many students might have attained at or above the average by the end of the four months, but a few very low scores pulled the average down. In such a case, the reasons for progress (or lack of progress) may not be apparent. How much of the result was due to the quality of the programme, the fidelity of delivery of the programme (was it taught as its authors intended?) and the motivation of the students? Add in a single test being used to establish baseline, with the possibility that some students might not have actually needed the intervention in the first place, and the results become very difficult to interpret in this form. As a result, a rigorous evaluation of results will need to explore the progress of each student in order to be useful.

This brings us to the second way to evaluate progress. In interventions,

94  Brooks, G. (2016). *What works for children and young people with literacy difficulties? The effectiveness of literacy schemes* (5th ed.). Dyslexia-SpLD Trust.

especially those for students who are reading well behind their peers, it is important to use single-case designs.[95] This means that each student's progress is tracked separately within the intervention, and monitored lesson by lesson. Where the student's progress stalls, the teacher can analyse error patterns and adjust the programme immediately. If interventions are designed to be run in this way, senior leaders can see individual results transparently at any time during the intervention. In other words, if individual daily measures are used, teachers can make adjustments to help students immediately, programmes continue to have impact, and senior leaders can easily see how much impact they are having. At the same time, aggregating the results is simple.

At this point it should be apparent that a great deal of emphasis has been placed upon staff expertise. We have to accept that as a profession, we have often asked those with the least qualifications and experience to support those students with the greatest difficulties. We have also expected that complex learning needs can be addressed without a high level of training, often because we are labouring under a misapprehension of 'higher-order' and 'lower-order' skills. What are often called 'lower-order' skills, we would call 'foundational' skills. Other 'higher-order' skills cannot exist without them. This does not mean that foundational skills are simple to teach, or that they matter less. It means that they matter more. If students have a strong set of foundational skills, they are easier to teach and indeed can often teach themselves. Students with an incomplete, fragmented set of foundational skills are unable to build anything reliable upon it. It is only once we accept that teaching foundational skills, such as decoding written text, requires at least as much systematic knowledge and pedagogical skill as teaching characterisation in Shakespeare that we will begin to train staff to the required levels to meet these students' needs.

To bring about such fundamental changes in the way teachers perceive these issues, senior leaders need to be supportive, determined and well-informed to build up their teams' subject knowledge and teaching

---

95   Alberto, P. A. & Troutman, A. C. (1986). *Applied behavior analysis for teachers* (2nd ed.). Columbus, OH: Merrill Publishing Company.

repertoire. Some staff may feel that they do not need to add to their training; some may feel threatened by the prospect; others may be overconfident and learn less than they should from the opportunities provided. The answer to all these attitudes, and indeed the driver for all training, is the school's mission. A key aspect of this mission is that every child should learn to read.

Once teachers embark on this mission, the complexity and challenge of the task opens up. Without answers, the field can seem intimidating; but the massive investment in research in the last 50 years means that there are indeed answers, even if they may not be the ones we expected or wanted. The drive of school leaders to communicate vision and mission is essential if we are to inspire and equip staff to achieve the goal. The implications are clear: school leaders can see that mission become a reality if we are well-informed, optimistic, willing to provide challenge, active in providing support, and rigorous in our self-evaluations.

The next chapter provides a more detailed investigation of what constitutes effective intervention, and how we should go about the tasks of choosing, implementing and evaluating appropriate programmes.

# Chapter 6:
# What does it take for effective reading intervention at secondary school?

*In New Zealand, in the early 2000s, we attended a compulsory professional development session. After the presentation, the floor was opened for questions.*

*'Your talk on the importance of developing higher consciousness in teachers and students in order to lead them to a more mindful state has been interesting,' I said, 'but can you tell us about the research base for the meditation practices you are recommending?'*

*'I'm glad you asked me that,' the presenter replied smoothly. 'In fact, there is a very solid base of research. Our founder developed his ideas by spending eight weeks in a flotation tank.'*

## Teachers and research

For a long time the relationship between teaching and research was fairly simple: teachers taught and academics did research. There was little or no interaction between the two groups. From the 1980s, the profile of research began to change – not because of a growing interest in research methods, but because educational fads began to appear in education around the world, and these fads claimed to be supported by 'research'. Such fads had intuitive appeal, and claims that research 'showed' them to be effective in boosting pupils' learning went largely uncontested. Very few teachers knew much about research, and so they were in no position to either challenge or evaluate the claims. It was also at this time that calls for greater impact in education were heard in many countries. Translated through the prism of politics, the result was structural changes which relied heavily on making managers more powerful, but also more accountable. This, it was argued, would put incentives for positive change in place, and would result in higher standards overall.

While standards did rise in many respects, the new powers unleashed a wave of fads upon teaching. Managers were now in a position to direct teaching styles, curriculum content, and staff training far more so than they had been. But these same managers were implementing 'innovations' which they had no capacity to evaluate, since they were without the necessary education and training. In turn, these managers promoted other teachers on the basis of their enthusiasm for such changes.

One example of a long-lasting education fad is the visual-auditory-kinaesthetic 'learning styles' myth. Research from as long ago as the 1990s found that there was no significant evidence of impact, but uninteresting truth does not travel as quickly as interesting lies, and it was still common practice for school inspectors in the UK to be judging lessons based on the quality of VAK provision in the classroom in 2010. Another 'fake news' story in education was the idea that the brain could be rewired to improve learning through physical exercises such as balancing on wobble-boards and 'crossing the mid-line'. In one primary school we encountered, the entire literacy support system was replaced by a 'sensory motor programme' involving exercises like those above. The fact that there was no scientific support for such practices did not stop uninformed school leaders from imposing them on their students and staff. A current example in many schools is the use of coloured paper backgrounds, coloured overlays and coloured spectacle lenses to improve student reading. In one school visited recently, there were seven different paper colours listed for different students' exam papers. Such practices are without scientific support, despite what their practitioners may claim.[96]

In the field of reading interventions, evidence of effectiveness ran a distant fourth behind whether an intervention intuitively appealed to teachers and managers, how easy it was to deliver, and how much students 'engaged' with it. Teachers researched neither the underlying theoretical constructs nor the evidence for derived teaching approaches, and as a result were left at the mercy of the claims (no doubt enthusiastic and well-intentioned) of the authors or publishers.

In recent years the landscape has begun to change significantly. There is now much more talk about research and evaluation of evidence for interventions and teaching approaches. However, because so few teachers have training in this area, and because they have so little time to do their own investigations, the control of information has shifted to what might be called 'research clearinghouses' which effectively act as consumer guides, testing and comparing interventions, weighing up the security of the evidence, and making recommendations about value for money.

Admittedly, this is an improvement on what went before – but it is far from ideal. Teachers are still reliant on others to make judgements and recommendations, and there is good evidence that these clearinghouses are themselves vulnerable to bias and selectivity. What Works Clearinghouse, the US government's flagship publicly funded organisation, has been criticised for apparently arbitrary criteria for including or excluding studies in its reports.[97] This, it is claimed, has led to a misrepresentation of the strength of evidence in favour of particular interventions – for example, by excluding all studies conducted before a certain date, regardless of quality. In some cases, only evidence from

---

96  Hyatt, K. J. (2010). Irlen tinted lenses and overlays. *MUSEC Briefings 22*. Retrieved from auspeld.org.au/wp-content/uploads/2014/08/Irlen-Lenses-and-Overlays-MUSEC-Briefing.pdf

97  Engelmann, S. (2003). Machinations of What Works Clearinghouse. Retrieved from www.zigsite.com/PDFs/MachinationsWWC%28V4%29.pdf

randomised controlled trials (RCTs) is included in reports. While RCTs are indeed a high-level test of effectiveness (if well-designed and carefully implemented) they are by no means the only kind of evidence that should be considered by research consumers. Indeed, without a trail of other kinds of evidence, it is much more difficult, if not impossible, to design useful RCTs. And of course, there are the more subtle kinds of biases, where certain approaches are favoured for further research and funding, or where sympathetic headlines are written which turn out to be unjustified by a study's results.

To navigate this environment, teachers and especially school leaders must have a sound knowledge of research methods, how to interpret and evaluate studies, and the strengths and potential biases of organisations which act as research gatekeepers. This assertion may alarm leaders who are already overstretched – but there is no alternative. This is how we will keep our profession – and our students – safe from being exploited by fads and uninformed innovation. Rest assured, human nature being what it is, that there will continue to be a stream of 'innovations' on offer. There is no way around it: we will only advance teaching to have more impact by being more scientific about what we do and how we do it. The irony is that equipping teachers in this way will free up students and staff to be more creative and genuinely innovative.

In this chapter we are going to look more deeply into the business of evaluating interventions, what the research has to tell us, and what to bear in mind when implementing interventions in secondary schools.

## Problems with interventions and why, so often, they don't seem to work

It is rare to hear of an intervention that has a dramatic effect. For the most part, we see a slight effect on student performance, but we have the satisfaction of knowing that 'we did what we could'. In the last chapter we talked about challenging a culture of low expectations in terms of what students can be expected to achieve. In this section, we will look at what limits the effectiveness of reading interventions.

## Low expectations

One of the common (and incorrect) assumptions about educational achievement is that a 'normal distribution', or 'bell curve', means that a certain percentage will do badly. Because this system is used to moderate the results of formal examinations (for example, at GCSE in England), we extrapolate backwards. Standardised tests of reading are particularly prone to producing this kind of expectation, where the average score of children of a certain age becomes their 'reading age'. It therefore seems logical to conclude that 'the bell curve' determines that some children must be poor readers.

However, in the real world, reading is not about a statistical distribution; it is about practical necessity. If students have fallen behind their peers, then a standardised test is a useful indicator to warn us of a problem. But it does not enable them to prepare for the world; that is the job of schools, not of standardised tests. As Alison Clarke has pointed out, our response should be to move the whole bell curve so that all students, even those at the lower end of the distribution, are capable readers. Although this means that some students at the upper end will be even more exceptional, we should not be deterred.

Another reason that we expect little from interventions is that we assume that the children in them are suffering from a disability of some kind. Because of this assumption, we believe that any intervention will struggle to produce results. But the point of intervention is to do what regular classroom teaching cannot. Yes, there will always be people who find reading much more difficult than others; but well-designed intervention should be able to address these difficulties.

Under such conditions, interventions with little or no impact are run year after year in our schools. This comes with costs – not merely in licences, salaries and staff time, but also in student time and student morale.

## Lack of fidelity

One of the greatest threats to advancing education scientifically is the issue of fidelity. We now routinely evaluate interventions, but rarely question our own approach to fidelity of delivery. In the hectic pace of school life, it is easy to approach new teaching approaches, or interventions, superficially. We cut corners from the original approach, make a few 'adjustments' and 'adapt to our context' (which often means 'our timetable'). Then we wonder why it's 'not working' – why we see less student engagement than expected, why there doesn't seem to be much academic progress.

Training to a high level is therefore essential if we are to deliver with fidelity, and this includes understanding the underlying methodology. This matters because it helps us to understand why certain elements are arranged as they are. Does it really matter if two components are switched? I recall observing one reading tutor who had changed the order of the lesson plan she had been trained to use. When asked why she did this, she simply said that she preferred to start the lesson at a different point. She had forgotten that it mattered to start the lesson with previous learning (for revision, early success, and motivation) rather than new learning. Schools are often reluctant to invest limited resources in training, but trying to implement a high-quality intervention without proper staff development is effectively a waste of money: 'The careful training, implementation, supervision and monitoring which characterises research studies may not always be observed in other circumstances with detrimental effects on the outcome of the intervention (Byrne & Fielding-Barnsley, 1995; Byrne *et al*, 2010; see Carter & Wheldall, 2008 for further discussion of this issue).'[98]

One of the biggest threats to fidelity of delivery is what has become known as the Dunning-Kruger Effect.[99] We feel confident that we

---

98  Hempenstall, K. (2017). Older students' literacy problems. Retrieved from www. nifdi.org/news-latest-2/blog-hempenstall/407-older-students-literacy-problems.

99  Kruger, J. & Dunning, D. (1999). Unskilled and unaware of it: how difficulties in recognizing one's own incompetence lead to inflated self-assessments. *Journal of Personality and Social Psychology, 77*(6), 1121–1134. dx.doi.org/10.1037/0022-3514.77.6.1121

have mastered something only because we are such novices that we don't know how much we still have to learn. Early success can convince us that we know enough to tinker, and that can ultimately have negative consequences. If we persevere with learning more about an approach, we steadily learn more and more about how much we don't know. We may well find that we have skills yet to be learned which, when we set out, we didn't even know existed.

**Lack of sophistication**

A third reason for interventions having a poor track record is that many have lacked sophistication. Single-dimension reading programmes, such as a phonics-only intervention, will not do the job at secondary school. Boardman *et al* point out that struggling adolescent readers need input in at least five areas (with the possible addition of phonics if indicated): vocabulary, fluency, word study, comprehension and motivation.[100] Interventions which attempt to circumvent or address these issues in a token way are likely to fail. Secondary reading interventions need to be sophisticated and this involves significant staff training, especially around managing motivation. After all, if you have reached secondary school and you haven't succeeded in reading after six years or more of education, you are not going to be motivated to read – in fact, you will have strong motivations to avoid doing so.

A related issue is that of a simplistic underlying construct of reading. Reading research shows that the processes in developing immediate word recognition and fluent reading of connected text are complex, involving cognitive processes linked to phonology, orthographic recognition, memory, lexical distinctions, spelling probabilities, verbal reasoning, background knowledge, to name a selection.[101] Where the underlying assumptions of the theory are limited (*eg*

100 Boardman, A. G., Roberts, G., Vaughn, S., Wexler, J., Murray, C. S., & Kosanovich, M. (2008). *Effective instruction for adolescent struggling readers: a practice brief.* Portsmouth, NH: RMC Research Corporation, Center on Instruction.
101 Kilpatrick, D. A. (2015). *Essentials of assessing, preventing, and overcoming reading difficulties.* Hoboken, NJ: John Wiley & Sons.

the student just needs to memorise the appearance of the word) the intervention may demand great effort but provide very little payoff. This will quickly show in a decline in student motivation. After all, we know when we are learning and we know when we are failing.

## Insufficient quality of assessment

In the section on screening in the last chapter, we outlined the importance of thorough data to enable us to identify those who need support, and to identify the areas in which they need that help. Once identified for intervention, however, further diagnostic assessment needs to be carried out. In our intervention, we complete two exhaustive assessments at the word and sentence level (spread out over several sessions) in order to identify the content that needs to be taught and mastered. Insufficient assessment can result not only in students being misplaced but also in them being taught material that they already know, or not being taught information that they needed.

Assessment of the impact of teaching has to be built into every lesson – not only for accountability purposes, but also so that we can make the necessary adjustments to the programme to meet the student's needs as they become apparent. For example, if a student needs more practice on a sound-spelling item, our teaching records should enable us to identify this. If a student is stalled at a certain level of fluency, we should be able to spot this quickly and provide appropriate practice to help them increase their read-aloud rate. Intervention design without inbuilt data collection at every step of the lesson is unlikely to be effective, as learning problems will be missed, and the effects of unresolved problems compound as students work through a programme.

## Assumptions and intuitions rather than data

Instead of reliable assessment data, staff delivering interventions may rely on assumptions or intuitions about students' capabilities or readiness to progress. Often this is labelled as 'professional judgement'. Thus, we have seen a student held back from advancement because staff felt he was 'not quite ready yet'. On checking the student's reading data, we found that he had indeed mastered previous learning, to the point where he should have been reading at a more challenging level. Conversely, we have seen a student advanced because a tutor felt that she had a good grasp of what she had read – but the criteria for advancement had not been met, and as a result the student had failed on her post-test at the end of the programme. Good intervention design provides objective criteria for advancement or 'slicing back' to practise component skills.

**Time cost**

As teachers we frequently bemoan the pressures on our time, but it is perhaps surprising that we are much less jealous of students' time. Students in the UK have 950 hours of curriculum time per year, covering 10, 11, or 12 subjects. Subjects with the greatest number of hours will see their students for just four hours per week, or 160 hours over the year. Interventions that can cut into this very limited time must have a powerful payoff which allows students greater access to the curriculum than they had before. We have seen students in interventions for up to 20% of their school week, discouraged by the separation from their peers and its associated stigma, and making little or no progress. Intervention design should be short, intense and limit impact on curriculum time.

**Impact of ineffective interventions on students**

Experiencing a series of ineffective interventions over the years can have seriously detrimental effects on students. First, it creates an aversion to reading, since reading comes to be seen as an activity in which failure is inevitable. Secondly, the student tends to see him or herself as lacking intelligence. This discouragement, and the associated belief that the student cannot learn, gradually seeps into other areas of the curriculum, affecting cognition, motivation and behaviour[102] with compounding effects on mental health, confidence and self-esteem.[103]

In summary, where there has been a track record of ineffective interventions (and in our experience, this is widespread), school systems have actually weakened student achievement and made it more difficult for poor readers to succeed. This would be depressing, but fortunately, scientific research has contributed enormously to our theoretical and practical knowledge in this field, so that we now have a very good idea of what constitutes an effective reading intervention at secondary school.

*With a reading age of seven and a half years in Year 9, Saffron was timetabled to begin lessons in the Literacy Centre. She had already had two years of one-to-one reading intervention elsewhere in the school, but had made no progress. She was quiet and timid, and the learning support staff I spoke to about her told me I would 'be lucky – she doesn't remember anything. It just goes in one ear and out the other.'*

*Saffron did have low comprehension, and she was very anxious. She was making slow progress, so in order to build her fluency in sub-skills, we 'sliced back' to develop her phonemic awareness, with oral segmenting and blending, and discrimination of sound changes between nonsense words. It was a challenge: some sequences required five attempts before she was able to master the different discriminations. There were times when I wondered, 'Are you going to be the student I can't teach?' – but, after ten weeks, Saffron had mastered all the sub-skills. Was it worth the effort? Absolutely! When we returned to Thinking Reading lessons, Saffron made steady progress, and after 48 lessons had caught up completely in her reading. She had progressed at a rate of 1.9 months per lesson, and gained 7.5 years to be reading at a 15-year-old level.*

---

102 Stanovich, K. E. (1986). Matthew effects in reading: some consequences of individual differences in the acquisition of literacy. *Reading Research Quarterly, 21*(4), 360–407. Retrieved from www.keithstanovich.com/Site/Research_on_Reading_files/RRQ86A.pdf

103 Hempenstall, K. (2016). Literacy and behaviour. Retrieved from: www.nifdi.org/news-latest-2/blog-hempenstall/405-literacy-and-behaviour

*However, although her comprehension had improved, she still needed support, so she went on to complete an intensive comprehension programme in a small group.*

*When we last saw her, she was reading the prologue of Shakespeare's* Romeo and Juliet *out loud to her English class.*

## What is required for an effective intervention?

For some years there was limited research available on what constituted effective intervention with secondary school students with reading difficulties. This is changing, and there is now growing interest in the area. This is no small matter: if society, through secondary schools, takes the opportunity to address deep-seated literacy problems while students are still at school, we can ease many social problems, improve our citizens' quality of life, and improve productivity in our economies. That said, the work involved in addressing these problems is not easy, and there are many barriers to overcome.

## The complexity of addressing reading problems at secondary school

Jeanne Chall, the eminent reading researcher, distinguished 'learning to read' in the earlier years of primary education from 'reading to learn' for the years following.[104] This distinction is widely accepted[105; 106; 107] and is crucial to designing instruction for students in these later years of education. In addition to phonic knowledge, the demands of subject learning at secondary school require specific knowledge in order to facilitate comprehension, specific vocabulary to mediate domain-specific knowledge, and fluency in order to assimilate content and develop more complex academic skills.

---

104 Chall, J. S. & Jacobs, V. A. (1983). Writing and reading in the elementary grades: developmental trends among low SES children. *Language Arts, 60*(5), 617–626.

105 Stanovich, K. E. (1986). Matthew effects in reading: some consequences of individual differences in the acquisition of literacy.

106 Boardman, A. G., Roberts, G., Vaughn, S., Wexler, J., Murray, C. S., & Kosanovich, M. (2008). *Effective instruction for adolescent struggling readers: a practice brief.*

107 Hempenstall, K. (2013). A history of disputes about reading instruction. Retrieved from www.nifdi.org/news-latest-2/blog-hempenstall/396-a-history-of-disputes-about-reading-instruction

These additional demands do not make phonics any less important. Phonics – how the written code represents the spoken code of English – is an essential foundation for understanding what is on the page. The problems caused by the guessing strategies of whole language, which seek to substitute inference from context for actual decoding skills, are well documented elsewhere. Suffice to say that 20% of those arriving at secondary have been failed by insufficient teaching and need help to catch up fast. Some of that help will involve repairing a lack of phonics knowledge; but along with that deficit, other deficits in comprehension, vocabulary and general knowledge have followed and accumulated – the so-called 'Matthew effect'.[108]

> In a report to the Office of Educational Research and Improvement, Snow (2002) noted that US students are falling behind students in other comparable countries because underdeveloped basic skills limit their attainment in the challenging subject-specific demands of the secondary school curriculum.[109]

## The five strands of reading

In one of the largest meta-analyses of reading instruction, the National Reading Panel identified five key areas that students need to master to become successful readers:[110]

- Phonemic awareness: The ability to hear and identify individual sounds in spoken words.

- Phonics: The relationship between the letters of written language and the sounds of spoken language.

- Fluency: The capacity to read text accurately and quickly.

- Vocabulary: All the words students must know to communicate effectively.

108 Stanovich, K. E. (1986). Matthew effects in reading: some consequences of individual differences in the acquisition of literacy.
109 Hempenstall, K. (2013). Literacy assessment based upon the National Reading Panel's Big Five components. Retrieved from www.nifdi.org/news-latest-2/blog-hempenstall/393-literacy-assessment-based-upon-the-national-reading-panel-s-big-five-components
110 Learning Point Associates. (2004). *A closer look at the five essential components of effective reading instruction: a review of scientifically based reading research for teachers.* Retrieved from files.eric.ed.gov/fulltext/ED512569.pdf

- Comprehension: The ability to understand what has been read.[109]

In an important follow-up to the NRP's 2000 report, Camilli, Vargas and Yurecko attempted a replication of the original study. They concluded that while teaching systematic phonics was still important, when combined with structured language teaching and with effective one-to-one tutoring, an effect size *three times as large* could be achieved.[111]

Boardman *et al*, in their excellent overview *Effective instruction for adolescent struggling readers: a practice brief,* argue that we should adjust the focus for older students:

> Instructional recommendations for older readers differ only slightly from those for younger readers. They can be organised into five general areas:
>
> - word study;
> - fluency;
> - vocabulary;
> - comprehension; and
> - motivation.

The authors go on to explain:

> Absent from this list are phonemic awareness and phonics. For most older readers, instruction in advanced word study, or decoding multisyllabic words, is a better use of time than instruction in the more foundational reading skills (such as decoding single-syllable words) which many older readers have accomplished. Of course, we recognise that older readers possess a range of knowledge and skills, and there may be older readers who would profit from instruction in the more foundational skills. Because of the increased challenge of motivating older students and the positive reading outcomes associated with attending to student motivation to read, a section on motivation is also included.[112]

---

111 Camilli, G., Vargas, S., and Yurecko, M. (May 8, 2003). Teaching children to read: the fragile link between science and federal education policy. *Education Policy Analysis Archives, 11*(15). Retrieved from epaa.asu.edu/ojs/article/viewFile/243/369..

112 Boardman, A. G., Roberts, G., Vaughn, S., Wexler, J., Murray, C. S., & Kosanovich, M. (2008). *Effective instruction for adolescent struggling readers: a practice brief.*

In addition, careful, close assessment is a crucial prerequisite for effective teaching of reading.[108; 110; 112]

With that overview in mind, let us now explore the elements of effective intervention at secondary school.

## What the empirical research tells us that effective reading interventions need

### Detailed assessment

We have already touched on the importance of assessment for identification. While there is a general concern in education about over-testing of students, we are not concerned here with high-stakes testing or group ranking. Rather, we are concerned first with accurate identification of those in need of intervention, and secondly with ensuring that we have accurate information that will enable us to plan sharply targeted teaching. We need to find out exactly where students' knowledge gaps are, and ensure that these are filled. We need to make sure that we are not teaching material that the student already knows. We need to understand their levels of fluency and build these up to a practically useful level, both for long-term memory and for combining with other skills. And, as has been stated earlier, we need to know the domains of difficulty – decoding, comprehension, and/or motivation. Effective intervention will always rest on detailed assessment information, at the text, word, and sound-spelling levels.

### Stages of learning

We discussed stages of learning in Chapter 3. One of the main blockages to progress is not that children fail to learn when they are initially taught, but that they do not receive sufficient practice to become fluent in those same skills. Too often in education we think we have achieved our goal for students when they have become accurate; but actually, until students are fluent, they have not mastered the material. Another reason for entrenched difficulties is that students may have failed to acquire basic information, not because they were incapable of learning but because the presentation of the material was (to the student) ambiguous or confusing. The key teacher actions required at each stage of learning are:

- **Acquisition**: unambiguous presentation with guided practice and immediate feedback

- **Accuracy**: continued, spaced practice with a high accuracy criterion (usually 80–100%)

- **Fluency**: daily timed practice with carefully sequenced practice materials to a high rate per minute

- **Retention**: scheduled review of previously learned materials (spaced retrieval)

- **Generalisation**: practice in adapted contexts or in combining the target skills with other previously learned skills

- **Adaptation**: opportunities for independent, creative problem-solving

Effective intervention will make provision for addressing all of the first five stages.

### Attention to sub-skills or 'tool' skills

Integral to the stages of learning model is the assertion that the skills we perform on a regular basis – even those which we think of as basic – are in fact made up of many component skills. For example, walking requires coordination between the eyes and the limbs, coordination between arms and legs, proprioception (balance and orientation) and decision-making about direction and speed. When we break it down to this level, even tying a bow knot on a shoe is remarkably complex. When it comes to reading, the sub-skills are many and varied, and a lack of accuracy or fluency in any one can lead to difficulties. Effective assessment will be designed so that weaknesses in sub-skills can be rapidly identified and addressed. For example, we can check the student's fluency at reading oral prose and provide fluency exercises to build this up if they do not meet the minimum fluency criterion.

An enormous body of work has been collected on the fluency criteria students need to achieve in order for teachers to be confident of effective retention, and of successful combination with other skills. For example, Kubina (2002) provides an extensive list of fluency criteria for a wide range of tool skills. Johnson and Layng's classic 1992 paper, 'Breaking the structuralist barrier: literacy and numeracy with fluency', gives some striking examples of the power of fluency to enable 'curriculum leaps'.

> Haughton (personal communication, August 1978) found that college students having trouble in calculus could improve their performance by building fluency on very basic elements, such as saying and writing numbers and math facts. Haughton (1971, 1972, 1980) reported that a program of tool skill building improved underachieving students' math performance to the level of their competent peers, whereas an arbitrary reward system, increasing the potency of consequences, and extensive practice in math at the students' grade levels all failed to improve their performance. Again, the presenting problem is not always the problem to solve. ...

> Progress in complex tasks depends on high prerequisite skill performance. Our charts show us again and again that the higher the prerequisite skill rates, the faster a complex skill will be learned.[113]

**Carefully calibrated steps in learning**

There is another barrier to learning that students frequently encounter: the steps in the curriculum are too large – often because students lack the fluency in tool skills that teachers assume they possess. However, the difficulties associated with negotiating large steps in learning are particularly punishing for students with weak reading who are already struggling to keep up and whose motivation is suffering as a result. Effective intervention requires careful

---

113 Johnson, K. R. & Layng, T. V. J. (1992). Breaking the structuralist barrier: literacy and numeracy with fluency. *American Psychologist, 47*(11), 1475–1490.

calibration of content to ensure that each new step is achievable. This is consistent with Engelmann and Colvin's assertion with respect to Direct Instruction programmes that 'the amount of new information presented must be small enough that mastery could probably be induced in a few minutes'.[114] Planning to this level of detail is frequently absent from intervention programmes, many of which are presented as a resource for teachers rather than a carefully controlled procedure. The result is that students continue to struggle, and their learning problems remain unresolved. The level of detail to which the teaching material must be analysed by the programme designer is frequently underestimated.

## Phonic knowledge

Some students who struggle with reading at secondary do so because they have weak or faulty reasoning skills, their vocabulary is limited or they are dysfluent. These students may well have secure phonic knowledge and do not need intervention in this area. But there is a group of students, some of whom will also exhibit comprehension difficulties, who have significant gaps in their phonic knowledge. Assessment and identification processes should identify these students as early as possible. Despite the fact that they will likely possess their own idiosyncratic learning histories[97] (and are therefore likely to need one-to-one instruction), the body of knowledge that needs to be learned is finite and can be assessed and taught systematically.[115] Effective reading intervention at secondary school should provide for these students' needs.

## Vocabulary

Vocabulary building is an ongoing process which can be richly and successfully pursued in the regular classroom. In intervention, however, there is the opportunity to link vocabulary closely

114 Engelmann, S. & Colvin, G. (2006). Rubric for identifying authentic Direct Instruction programs. Retrieved from www.zigsite.com/PDFs/rubric.pdf
115 Moats, L. C. (1999). *Teaching reading is rocket science*. [PDF version]. American Federation of Teachers. Retrieved from www.aft.org/sites/default/files/reading_rocketscience_2004.pdf

with spelling and word study, and of course to close study of an appropriate portion of written text. Given that intervention time is likely to be limited, the focus for vocabulary teaching should be to ensure that students gain the knowledge they need to access the text that they are currently reading in the programme. There is of course also the possibility of setting additional independent work for students to develop independent reading and word-learning habits.

### Background knowledge

Intervention should broaden rather than restrict students' knowledge of the world. Reading a range of fiction and non-fiction texts at the student's current level, and ensuring that decoding and vocabulary learning is taught so that the student can extract meaning from the page, enables them to experience – often for the first time – the sense of empowerment and pleasure that comes from learning through reading. Using a range of texts about different domains – geography, astronomy, history, and biology, for example – is an opportunity to develop students' knowledge of the world. As this is one of the main goals of teaching children to read, interventions should be intentionally outward-looking in terms of reading subject matter.

### Comprehension

Whether the focus of the programme is decoding, comprehension, or both, the student must have the opportunity to demonstrate their understanding of what they have read. Comprehension is, of course, the goal of reading, and while there are many steps along the way, it is essential that students have the satisfaction of knowing that they have understood successfully. It is also essential for the teacher to know whether or not the student has understood, so that appropriate remedial action can be taken if necessary. For example, where students have improved their decoding knowledge and are fluent at their grade level, but have difficulties in comprehension, they can be allocated to a comprehension strategy intervention. Such instruction can be very effective over a relatively short time[116] and will support classroom work on background knowledge and vocabulary.

## Explicit language teaching

Sometimes referred to as 'word study', such instruction is designed to show students common syntactic and semantic relations between words. The study of verb inflections, prefixes, suffixes and other morphemes helps students to see that there are common patterns in English which enable them to deduce the meanings of unknown words. The suffix '-ment', for example, implies that a verb has been transformed into a noun ('government', 'adornment', 'alignment'). The study of word roots can include their etymology, and the use of what Boardman *et al* term 'additive instruction' to identify and link related groups of words.[112] For example, the terms 'hypothesis', 'synthesis' and 'antithesis' are all related through the root 'thesis'. Making these language patterns explicit for students requires both careful programme preparation and precise teaching presentation.

## Scheduling of programme components

We have looked at many of the components of effective intervention. However, some research indicates that the ways in which these components are arranged in an intervention can have a considerable impact on the students participating in the programme:

> Outcomes showed clearly that modality of instruction can matter considerably for these older struggling readers. The differences in gains clearly demonstrate that the Additive modality, with its sequential addition of each component (isolated phonological decoding instruction, followed by addition of spelling instruction, followed by addition of fluency instruction, and finally the addition of comprehension instruction) is potentially the best modality for remediating reading skills (decoding, spelling, fluency, comprehension) in older struggling readers. ... These students show

---

116 Willingham, D. T. (Winter 2006/07). Ask the cognitive scientist: the usefulness of brief instruction in reading comprehension strategies. *American Educator, 30*(4), 39–45, 50.

that they are highly sensitive to the scheduling of the components and the amounts of instructional time per component.[117]

Note that the sensitivity to scheduling applies to adolescent struggling readers.

Calhoon and Petscher found compelling indications that the level of improvement by their adolescent sample and the percentages of students classified as gainers were influenced by the way that elements of how a common curriculum were organized and sequenced during instruction.[118]

Some of this effect appears to be related to developing tool skills to accuracy and fluency. Other elements may well be linked to motivation and students' sense of confidence and success.

**Motivation**

As Boardman *et al* point out, motivation is a particular concern with struggling older readers. A long history of difficulty with reading is likely to create a sense of aversion, and has negative impacts on self-esteem and confidence. It is therefore essential that interventions take this into account. One way of doing this is through programme design. There is a conventional idea in teaching that lessons should open with a 'hook' to engage students. The problem with this approach is that students quickly learn that after the first five minutes, lessons rarely continue to be as interesting as they appeared at first. In fact, in behavioural terms it is important to ensure that the first activity in the lesson is one which the student is familiar with and, while providing an element of challenge, has a high probability of success. This gives the student an early positive experience – essential for those with low motivation, and often high levels of anxiety, around reading.

---

117 Calhoon, M. B. & Petscher, Y. (2013). Individual and group sensitivity to remedial reading program design: examining reading gains across three middle school reading projects. *Reading and Writing: An Interdisciplinary Journal, 26*(4), 565–592.

118 Calhoon, M. B., Scarborough, H. S., & Miller, B. (2013). Interventions for struggling adolescent and adult readers: instructional, learner, and situational differences. *Reading and Writing: An Interdisciplinary Journal, 26*(4), 489–494.

Another area in which programmes should take account of student motivation is the length of each phase of the lesson. Practice activities should be timed and short. New learning activities should focus on a limited set of items with highly prescriptive teacher presentation to ensure efficiency and immediate success. Lastly, the Premack principle should be applied: the most interesting activities (such as reading new material) should be placed towards the end of the lesson to naturally reward the student's efforts.[119]

The other aspect of effective motivational management is the teacher's moment-by-moment interaction with the student. Effort, concentration and progress should be recognised and commented on. Such comments should be brief, specific and contingent: 'Well done on arriving so promptly. Let's get to work' or 'You concentrated really closely. Good effort.' Training and coaching in such motivational styles is very important to the success of interventions, but these needs are frequently overlooked by managers allocating staff. The area of motivation management is broad, complex and frequently misunderstood.

It cannot be overstated that children need effective teaching, not sympathy or disability-focused discourse that lowers expectations. Instead, teachers need training in skills like contingent reinforcement, behavioural observations, analysing behavioural contingencies, reinforcement schedules, fading, prompting, antecedent control, and effective use of feedback – to name but a selection of the possibilities.

## Summary

There is now a wealth of research on reading. The literature on effective interventions for adolescents was once limited, but has been growing in recent years. This chapter has concentrated on those areas where the research is converging around practical solutions and has been based on our own experience of intervening with struggling readers at secondary school. Our conclusions are:

119 Alberto, P. A. & Troutman, A. C. (1986). *Applied behavior analysis for teachers* (2nd ed.). Columbus, OH: Merrill Publishing Company, p. 202.

- Effective programme design is highly complex and good results cannot be achieved without it.

- The level of training required to implement effective programmes is extensive, and taking shortcuts in this area wastes student time and school resources. Better to do it properly or not at all.

- 'Not at all' is not actually an option, because schools have a moral obligation to ensure that all students are able to read at a level appropriate to their age by the time they complete their compulsory education.

## What Next?

The aim of this chapter has been to provide an overview of the critical factors in successfully choosing and implementing an effective reading intervention at secondary school. However, having absorbed this information, the next question is: what comes next? How do we translate these thoughts into effective actions? Here are seven practical steps to consider:

1. Make a decision as a school community to ensure that no student leaves school unable to read at their age level.

2. Review the whole school curriculum to ensure that it both challenges strong readers and supports students with reading difficulties.

3. Train school staff to spot and respond appropriately when students are being held back by reading problems in the regular classroom.

4. Review the impact of current reading interventions.

5. Put a comprehensive screening system in place.

6. Limit interventions to those which meet student needs and are based upon sound, research-evidenced methods.

7. Put in place an evaluation cycle to ensure that these interventions continue to increase in impact.

# Afterword

Hopefully by now you have caught the vision: we can teach virtually all students to read. This does not mean that they will all be equally good, but it should mean that after receiving an education, everyone will be able to read the newspaper, apply for a job, read the instructions on their medicine bottles, and read something for enjoyment.

One of the great afflictions of education is the seductive language around 'intelligence' which distracts us from our core business. We believe that as teachers, our job is not to establish a student's 'potential', but to move them onwards from wherever they may be. In other words, the focus should be on the quality of our instruction, not on students' 'ability' or 'disability'. No doubt there are hereditary and environmental factors at work for all of us as we learn and grow; but the teacher's concern should be to develop a repertoire of skills and tools to ensure that any student can improve from their current level of performance.

For the last 15 years we have worked to develop a set of tools that can be applied to maximum effect on students' reading. That work has been informed by research every step of the way, and we have seen the results – not only on students' reading, but on their self-esteem, confidence and motivation. There is a sense in which nothing in Thinking Reading is original – everything has been drawn from published, publicly available research. We stand, as they say, on the shoulders of giants.

We do not claim that the solutions to long-standing educational problems are easy or that they can be attained without much effort. But thankfully, there have already been generations of teachers and researchers who have laboured long and faithfully to bring about the changes that are needed. To these often under-recognised colleagues, whose work we have drawn upon so often in these pages, we say a heartfelt thanks.

Lastly, our goal, and our hope for our readers, is to have an army of research-led teachers challenging myths and misconceptions, and promoting practices that have been validated by empirical research. If this book inspires readers to take up that challenge, then it has succeeded.

# Citations

**Introduction**

1. Inverness society for the education of the poor in the Highlands, Inverness, Scotland. (1826). *Moral statistics of the highlands and islands of Scotland.* Inverness: Education Society.

2. Murphy, J. (2014). On reading. Retrieved from horatiospeaks.wordpress. com/2014/11/23/330/.

**Chapter 1**

3. Moats, L. C. (1999). *Teaching reading is rocket science.* [PDF version]. American Federation of Teachers. Retrieved from www.aft.org/sites/default/files/reading_rocketscience_2004.pdf

4. National Literacy Trust. (2014). *Read on. Get on. How reading can help children escape poverty.* Save the Children on behalf of the Read On. Get On. campaign. Retrieved from literacytrust.org.uk/documents/895/Read_On_Get_On_launch_report_2014.pdf

5. Cunningham, A. E. & Stanovich, K. E. (2001). What reading does for the mind. *American Educator, 22*(1–2), 8–15. Retrieved from www.aft.org/sites/default/files/periodicals/cunningham.pdf

6. Treffers-Daller, J. & Milton, J. (2013). Vocabulary size revisited: the link between vocabulary size and academic achievement. *Applied Linguistics Review, 4*(1), 151–172. ISSN 18686311 doi: doi.org/10.1515/applirev20130007 (Note: vocabulary estimates vary widely depending on the methodology used.)

7. Hempenstall, K. (2016). Literacy and behaviour. Retrieved from: www.nifdi.org/news-latest-2/blog-hempenstall/405-literacy-and-behaviour

8. Nicholson, T. (2015, November 12). Tom Nicholson: dyslexic kids need more than kind words. *The New Zealand Herald,* Retrieved from www.nzherald.co.nz/opinion/news/article.cfm?c_id=466&objectid=11544342

9.  Elliott, J. G. (2010). Dyslexia: diagnoses, debates and diatribes. *Education Canada, 46*(2), 14–17. Retrieved from www.edcan.ca/wp-content/uploads/EdCan-2006-v46-n2-Elliott.pdf

10. McGuiness, D. (2004). *Early reading instruction: what science really tells us about how to teach reading.* London: MIT Press.

11. National Literacy Trust. (2017). Adult literacy. Retrieved from literacytrust.org.uk/parents-and-families/adult-literacy/

12. Social Exclusion Unit. (2002). *Reducing re-offending by ex-prisoners.* Retrieved from www.bristol.ac.uk/poverty/downloads/keyofficialdocuments/Reducing%20Reoffending.pdf

13. National Council for Adult Learning. (2015). *Adult education facts that demand priority attention.* Retrieved from www.ncalamerica.org/AdultEDFacts&Figures1215.pdf

14. World Literacy Foundation. (2015). *The economic & social cost of illiteracy: a snapshot of illiteracy in a global context. Final report from the World Literacy Foundation.* Retrieved from worldliteracyfoundation.org/wp-content/uploads/2015/02/WLF-FINAL-ECONOMIC-REPORT.pdf

**Chapter 2**

15. Hempenstall, K. (2013). A history of disputes about reading instruction. Retrieved from www.nifdi.org/news-latest-2/blog-hempenstall/396-a-history-of-disputes-about-reading-instruction

16. Flesch, R. (1955). *Why Johnny can't read: and what you can do about it.* New York, NY: Harper and Row.

17. Chall, J. (1967). *Learning to read: the great debate.* New York, NY: McGraw-Hill.

18. Goodman, K. (1967). Reading: a psycholinguistic guessing game. *Journal of the Reading Specialist, 6*(4), 126–135. DOI: 10.1080/19388076709556976

19. Kozloff, M. (2002). A whole language catalogue of the grotesque. Retrieved from people.uncw.edu/kozloffm/wlquotes.html

20. Smith, F. (1975). *Comprehension and learning: a conceptual framework for teachers.* New York, NY: Holt, Rinehart and Winston.

21. Stanovich, K. E. (1993). Romance and reality. *The Reading Teacher, 47*(4), 280–291. Retrieved from www.keithstanovich.com/Site/Research_on_Reading_files/RdTch93.pdf

22. Kozloff, M. A., LaNunziata, L., & Cowardin, J. (1999). *Direct instruction in education.* Retrieved from www.beteronderwijsnederland.nl/files/active/0/Kozloff%20e.a.%20DI.pdf

23. Engelmann, S. (2004). Professional standards in education. Retrieved from zigsite.com/Standards.htm

24. Gough, P. B. & Tunmer, W. E. (1986). Decoding, reading, and reading disability. *Remedial and Special Education, 7*(1), 1–10.

25. Ehri, L. C. (2014). Orthographic mapping in the acquisition of sight word reading, spelling memory, and vocabulary learning. *Scientific Studies of Reading, 18*(1), 5–21. DOI: 10.1080/10888438.2013.819356

26. Kilpatrick, D. A. (2015). *Essentials of assessing, preventing, and overcoming reading difficulties.* Hoboken, NJ: John Wiley & Sons.

27. Taylor, J., David, M., & Rastle, K. (2017). Comparing and validating methods of reading instruction using behavioural and neural findings in an artificial orthography. *Journal of Experimental Psychology: General, 146*(6), 826–858.

28. Moats, L. C. (2007). *Whole language high jinks: how to tell when 'scientifically-based reading instruction- isn't.* Washington, DC: Thomas Fordham Foundation.

29. National Literacy Trust. (2014). *Read on. Get on. How reading can help children escape poverty.* Save the Children on behalf of the Read On. Get On. campaign. Retrieved from literacytrust.org.uk/documents/895/Read_On_Get_On_launch_report_2014.pdf

30. Moats, L. C. (1999). *Teaching reading is rocket science.* [PDF version]. American Federation of Teachers. Retrieved from www.aft.org/sites/default/files/reading_rocketscience_2004.pdf

31. Hempenstall, K. (2017). Older students' literacy problems. Retrieved from www.nifdi.org/news-latest-2/blog-hempenstall/407-older-students-literacy-problems

32. Tunmer, W. E., Chapman, J. W., Greaney, K. T., Prochnow, J. E., & Arrow, A. W. (2013). *Why the New Zealand national literacy strategy has failed and what can be done about it.* Massey University Institute of Education. Retrieved from www.massey.ac.nz/massey/fms/Massey%20News/2013/8/docs/Report-National-Literacy-Strategy-2013.pdf

33. McGrane, J., Stiff, J., Baird, J., Lenkeit, J., & Hopfenbeck, T. (2017). *Progress in international reading literacy study (PIRLS): national report for England.* Department for Education. Retrieved from www.gov.uk/government/uploads/system/uploads/attachment_data/file/664562/PIRLS_2016_National_Report_for_England-_BRANDED.pdf

34. Department for Education. (2015). *Reading: the next steps.* Retrieved from www.gov.uk/government/uploads/system/uploads/attachment_data/file/409409/Reading_the_next_steps.pdf

35. Goss, P. & Sonnemann, J. (2016, March). *Widening gaps: what NAPLAN tells us about student progress.* Carlton, VIC: Grattan Institute. Retrieved from grattan.edu.au/report/widening-gaps/

36. Kirsch, I. S., Jungeblut, A., Jenkins, L., & Kolstad, A. (2002). *Adult literacy in America: A first look at the findings of the National Adult Literacy Survey.* U.S. Department of Education. Retrieved from nces.ed.gov/pubs93/93275.pdf

37. Elliott, J. G. (2010). Dyslexia: diagnoses, debates and diatribes. *Education Canada*, *46*(2), 14–17. Retrieved from www.edcan.ca/wp-content/uploads/EdCan-2006-v46-n2-Elliott.pdf.

38. Stanovich, K. E. (1993). Does reading make you smarter? Literacy and the development of verbal intelligence. In H. Reese (Ed.), *Advances in child development and behavior, Vol. 24* (pp. 133–180). San Diego, CA: Academic Press. Retrieved from www.keithstanovich.com/Site/Research_on_Reading_files/Stanovich_Advances_1993.pdf

39. Barbash, S. (2012). *Clear teaching: with Direct Instruction, Siegfried Engelmann discovered a better way of teaching*. Education Consumers Foundation. Retrieved from education-consumers.org/pdf/CT_111811.pdf

40. Engelmann, S. (2010). Siegfried Engelmann 2: Improving the quality of learning. Retrieved from childrenofthecode.org/interviews/engelmann2.htm

41. Durham Unversity. (2014). The term 'dyslexia' is unscientific and misleading and should be abandoned, according to new book. Retrieved from www.dur.ac.uk/news/newsitem/?itemno=20285

42. Hyatt, K. J. (2010). Irlen tinted lenses and overlays. *MUSEC Briefings 22*. Retrieved from auspeld.org.au/wp-content/uploads/2014/08/Irlen-Lenses-and-Overlays-MUSEC-Briefing.pdf

43. Hempenstall, K. (2013). Keeping an eye on reading: is difficulty with reading a visual problem? Retrieved from www.nifdi.org/resources/news/hempenstall-blog/414-keeping-an-eye-on-reading-is-difficulty-with-reading-a-visual-problem

44. Binder, C. (1988). Precision teaching: measuring and attaining exemplary academic achievement. *Youth Policy, 10*(7), 12–15.

45. Hasbrouck, J. (2006). Drop everything and read – but how? *American Educator 30*(2). Retrieved from www.aft.org/periodical/american-educator/summer-2006/drop-everything-and-read-how

46. Henley, J. (2018, February 26). Icelandic language battles threat of 'digital extinction'. *The Guardian*, Retrieved from www.theguardian.com/world/2018/feb/26/icelandic-language-battles-threat-of-digital-extinction

**Chapter 3**

47. Kilpatrick, D. A. (2015). *Essentials of assessing, preventing, and overcoming reading difficulties*. Hoboken, NJ: John Wiley & Sons.

48. Tignor, R. L. (2011). *Egypt: a short history*. Princeton, NJ: Princeton University Press.

49. McGuiness, D. (2004). *Early reading instruction: what science really tells us about how to teach reading*. London: MIT Press.

50. Inverness society for the education of the poor in the Highlands, Inverness, Scotland. (1826). *Moral statistics of the highlands and islands of Scotland.* Inverness: Education Society.

51. McCrum, R., MacNeil, R., & Cran, W. (2011). *The story of English.* London: Faber & Faber.

52. Kameenui, E. J. & Simmons, D. C. (1990). *Designing instructional strategies: the prevention of academic learning problems.* Englewood Cliffs, NJ: Macmillan.

53. Moats, L. C. (2005/06). How spelling supports reading. *American Educator, 29*(4), 12–22; 42–43. Retrieved from www.aft.org/sites/default/files/periodicals/Moats. pdf

54. Kilpatrick, D. A. (2015). *Essentials of assessing, preventing, and overcoming reading difficulties.*

55. Barbash, S. (2012). *Clear teaching: with Direct Instruction, Siegfried Engelmann discovered a better way of teaching.* Education Consumers Foundation. Retrieved from education-consumers.org/pdf/CT_111811.pdf.

56. Moats, L. C. (1999). *Teaching reading is rocket science.* [PDF version]. American Federation of Teachers. Retrieved from www.aft.org/sites/default/files/reading_rocketscience_2004.pdf

57. Hempenstall, K. (2017). Feel like a spell? Effective spelling instruction. Retrieved from www.nifdi.org/resources/news/hempenstall-blog/390-feel-like-a-spell

58. Dehaene, S. (2011) *The massive impact of literacy on the brain and its consequences for education.* Human Neuroplasticity and Education. Pontifical Academy of Sciences, Scripta Varia 117, Vatican City 2011. Retrieved from www.pas.va/content/dam/accademia/pdf/sv117/sv117-dehaene.pdf

59. Clarke, A. (2015, May 11). *Preventing literacy failure and shifting the whole bell curve up* [Video]. Retrieved from www.youtube.com/watch?v=mafVooDom8k

60. Camilli, G., Vargas, S., & Yurecko, M. (2003) Teaching children to read: the fragile link between science and federal education policy. *Education Policy Analysis Archives, 11*(15). Retrieved from epaa.asu.edu/ojs/article/viewFile/243/369.

61. Moats, L. C. (1999). *Teaching reading is rocket science.*

62. Seidenberg, M. (2017). *Language at the speed of sight: how we read, why so many can't and what can be done about it.* New York, NY: Basic Books.

63. Moats, L. (2003). Teaching teachers to teach reading. Retrieved from www.childrenofthecode.org/interviews/moats.htm

64. Beck, I. L., McKeown, M. G., & Kucan, L. (2013*). Bringing words to life: robust vocabulary instruction.* New York, NY: The Guildford Press.

65. Lemov, D., Driggs, C., & Woolway, E. (2016). *Reading reconsidered: a practical guide to rigorous literacy instruction.* San Francisco, CA: Jossey-Bass.

66. Hart, B. & Risley, T. R. (1995). *Meaningful differences in the everyday experiences of young American children.* Baltimore, MD: P H Brookes.

67. Nation, I. S. P. (undated). *A brief critique of Hart, B. & Risley, T. (1995).* LALS, Victoria University of Wellington. Retrieved from www.victoria.ac.nz/lals/about/staff/publications/paul-nation/Hart_and_Risley_critique.pdf

68. Kilpatrick, D. A. (2015). *Essentials of assessing, preventing, and overcoming reading difficulties.* p. 282.

69. Cunningham, A. E. and Stanovich, K. E. (2001) What reading does for the mind. *Journal of Direct Instruction, 1*(2), 137–149.

70. Stanovich, K. E. (1986). Matthew effects in reading: some consequences of individual differences in the acquisition of literacy. *Reading Research Quarterly, 21*(4), 360–407. Retrieved from www.keithstanovich.com/Site/Research_on_Reading_files/RRQ86A.pdf

71. Beck, I. L., McKeown, M. G., & Kucan, L. (2013*). Bringing words to life: robust vocabulary instruction.* p. 83.

72. Boardman, A. G., Roberts, G., Vaughn, S., Wexler, J., Murray, C. S., & Kosanovich, M. (2008). *Effective instruction for adolescent struggling readers: a practice brief.* Portsmouth, NH: RMC Research Corporation, Center on Instruction.

73. White, O. R. & Haring, N. G. (1980). Exceptional teaching for exceptional children (2nd ed.). Columbus, OH: Merrill.

74. Lindsley, O. R. (1992). Precision teaching: discoveries and effects. *Journal of Applied Behaviour Analysis, 25*(1), 51–57.

75. Binder, C. (1988). Precision teaching: measuring and attaining exemplary academic achievement. *Youth Policy, 10*(7), 12–15.

76. Binder, C., Haughton, E., & Bateman, B. (2002). *Fluency: achieving true mastery in the learning process.* Retrieved from binde1.verio.com/wb_fluency.org/Publications/BinderHaughtonBateman2002.pdf

77. Kubina, R. M., Kostewicz, D. E., & Lin, F. (2009). The taxonomy of learning and behavioral fluency. *Journal of Precision Teaching and Celeration, 25,* 17–27. Retrieved from cdn2.hubspot.net/hubfs/3031078/Chartlytics_April2017/Docs/kubina_taxonomy_and_fluency.pdf?t=1494006957153

78. Ricketts, J., Sperring, R., & Nation, K. (2014). Educational attainment in poor comprehenders. *Frontiers in Psychology, 5,* Article 445, 1–11. Retrieved from www.frontiersin.org/articles/10.3389/fpsyg.2014.00445/full

**Chapter 4**

79. Stothard, S., Snowling, M., & Hulme, C. (2009). *The rate and identification of reading difficulties in secondary school pupils in England.* York:University of York; London: GL Assessment Limited.

80. Johnson, R. T. & Johnson, D. W. (2002). *An overview of cooperative learning.* Retrieved from digsys.upc.es/ed/general/Gasteiz/docs_ac/Johnson_Overview_of_Cooperative_Learning.pdf

81. Beck, I. L., McKeown, M. G., & Kucan, L. (2013*). Bringing words to life: robust vocabulary instruction.* New York, NY: The Guildford Press. p. 83.

82. Heron, T. E., Okyere, B. A., & Miller, A. D. (1991). A taxonomy of approaches to teach spelling. *Journal of Behavioral Education, 1*(1), 117–130. Retrieved from link. springer.com/article/10.1007/BF00956757

83. Matthews, P. H. (2014). *The concise Oxford dictionary of linguistics.* Oxford: OUP.

84. Willingham, D. T. (Winter 2006/07). Ask the cognitive scientist: the usefulness of brief instruction in reading comprehension strategies. *American Educator, 30*(4), 39–45, 50.

## Chapter 5

85. Hempenstall, K. (2016). Literacy and behaviour. Retrieved from: www.nifdi.org/news-latest-2/blog-hempenstall/405-literacy-and-behaviour

86. Lemov, D., Driggs, C., & Woolway, E. (2016). *Reading reconsidered: a practical guide to rigorous literacy instruction.* San Francisco, CA: Jossey-Bass.

87. Beck, I. L., McKeown, M. G., & Kucan, L. (2013*). Bringing words to life: robust vocabulary instruction.* New York, NY: The Guildford Press.

88. Rose, N. J. (2014). Growth mindset: it's not magic. Retrieved from evidenceintopractice.wordpress.com/2014/06/01/growth-mindset-its-not-magic/

89. Gorard, S., Siddiqui, N., & See, B. H. (2015). *Accelerated Reader.* Education Endowment Foundation and Durham University. Retrieved from v1.educationendowmentfoundation.org.uk/uploads/pdf/Accelerated_Reader_(Final).pdf

90. Barbash, S. (2012). *Clear teaching: with Direct Instruction, Siegfried Engelmann discovered a better way of teaching.* Education Consumers Foundation. Retrieved from education-consumers.org/pdf/CT_111811.pdf.

91. Moats, L. C. (1999). *Teaching reading is rocket science.* [PDF version]. American Federation of Teachers. Retrieved from www.aft.org/sites/default/files/reading_rocketscience_2004.pdf

92. Vellutino, F. R., Fletcher, J. M., Snowling, M. J., and Scanlon, D. M. (2004). Specific reading disability (dyslexia): what have we learned in the past four decades? *Journal of Child Psychology and Psychiatry, 45*(1), 2–40.

93. Vaughn, S. & Fletcher, J. M. (2012). Response to intervention with secondary school students with reading difficulties. *Journal of Learning Disabilities, 45*(3), 244–256. Retrieved from www.ncbi.nlm.nih.gov/pmc/articles/PMC3356920/

94. Brooks, G. (2016). *What works for children and young people with literacy difficulties? The effectiveness of literacy schemes* (5th ed.). Dyslexia-SpLD Trust.

95. Alberto, P. A. & Troutman, A. C. (1986). *Applied behavior analysis for teachers* (2nd ed.). Columbus, OH: Merrill Publishing Company.

**Chapter 6**

96. Hyatt, K. J. (2010). Irlen tinted lenses and overlays. *MUSEC Briefings 22*. Retrieved from auspeld.org.au/wp-content/uploads/2014/08/Irlen-Lenses-and-Overlays-MUSEC-Briefing.pdf

97. Engelmann, S. (2003). Machinations of What Works Clearinghouse. Retrieved from www.zigsite.com/PDFs/MachinationsWWC%28V4%29.pdf

98. Hempenstall, K. (2017). Older students' literacy problems. Retrieved from www. nifdi.org/news-latest-2/blog-hempenstall/407-older-students-literacy-problems.

99. Kruger, J. & Dunning, D. (1999). Unskilled and unaware of it: how difficulties in recognizing one's own incompetence lead to inflated self-assessments. *Journal of Personality and Social Psychology, 77*(6), 1121–1134. dx.doi.org/10.1037/0022-3514.77.6.1121

100. Boardman, A. G., Roberts, G., Vaughn, S., Wexler, J., Murray, C. S., & Kosanovich, M. (2008). *Effective instruction for adolescent struggling readers: a practice brief.* Portsmouth, NH: RMC Research Corporation, Center on Instruction.

101. Kilpatrick, D. A. (2015). *Essentials of assessing, preventing, and overcoming reading difficulties.*

102. Stanovich, K. E. (1986). Matthew effects in reading: some consequences of individual differences in the acquisition of literacy. *Reading Research Quarterly, 21*(4), 360–407. Retrieved from www.keithstanovich.com/Site/Research_on_Reading_files/RRQ86A.pdf

103. Hempenstall, K. (2016). Literacy and behaviour. Retrieved from: www.nifdi.org/news-latest-2/blog-hempenstall/405-literacy-and-behaviour

104. Chall, J. S. & Jacobs, V. A. (1983). Writing and reading in the elementary grades: developmental trends among low SES children. *Language Arts, 60*(5), 617–626.

105. Stanovich, K. E. (1986). Matthew effects in reading: some consequences of individual differences in the acquisition of literacy.

106. Boardman, A. G., Roberts, G., Vaughn, S., Wexler, J., Murray, C. S., & Kosanovich, M. (2008). *Effective instruction for adolescent struggling readers: a practice brief.*

107. Hempenstall, K. (2013). A history of disputes about reading instruction. Retrieved from www.nifdi.org/news-latest-2/blog-hempenstall/396-a-history-of-disputes-about-reading-instruction.

108. Stanovich, K. E. (1986). Matthew effects in reading: some consequences of individual differences in the acquisition of literacy.

109. Hempenstall, K. (2013). *Literacy assessment based upon the National Reading Panel's Big Five components. Retrieved from www.nifdi.org/news-latest-2/blog-hempenstall/393-literacy-assessment-based-upon-the-national-reading-panel-s-big-five-components*

110. Learning Point Associates. (2004). *A closer look at the five essential components of effective reading instruction: a review of scientifically based reading research for teachers.* Retrieved from files.eric.ed.gov/fulltext/ED512569.pdf

111. Camilli, G., Vargas, S., & Yurecko, M. (2003) Teaching children to read: the fragile link between science and federal education policy. *Education Policy Analysis Archives, 11*(15). Retrieved from epaa.asu.edu/ojs/article/viewFile/243/369.

112. Boardman, A. G., Roberts, G., Vaughn, S., Wexler, J., Murray, C. S., & Kosanovich, M. (2008). *Effective instruction for adolescent struggling readers: a practice brief.*

113. Johnson, K. R. & Layng, T. V. J. (1992). Breaking the structuralist barrier: literacy and numeracy with fluency. *American Psychologist, 47*(11), 1475–1490.

114. Engelmann, S. & Colvin, G. (2006). Rubric for identifying authentic Direct Instruction programs. Retrieved from www.zigsite.com/PDFs/rubric.pdf

115. Moats, L. C. (1999). *Teaching reading is rocket science.* [PDF version]. American Federation of Teachers. Retrieved from www.aft.org/sites/default/files/reading_rocketscience_2004.pdf

116. Willingham, D. T. (Winter 2006/07). Ask the cognitive scientist: the usefulness of brief instruction in reading comprehension strategies. *American Educator, 30*(4), 39–45, 50.

117. Calhoon, M. B., & Petscher, Y. (2013). Individual and group sensitivity to remedial reading program design: examining reading gains across three middle school reading projects. *Reading and Writing: An Interdisciplinary Journal, 26*(4), 565–592.

118. Calhoon, M. B., Scarborough, H. S., & Miller, B. (2013). Interventions for struggling adolescent and adult readers: instructional, learner, and situational differences. *Reading and Writing: An Interdisciplinary Journal, 26*(4), 489–494.

119. Alberto, P. A. & Troutman, A. C. (1986). *Applied behavior analysis for teachers* (2nd ed.). Columbus, OH: Merrill Publishing Company.

# Appendix: phonemic transcription chart

### Vowels

| i:<br>fleece | ɪ<br>kit | ʊ<br>foot | u:<br>goose | ɪə<br>near | eɪ<br>face | X |
|---|---|---|---|---|---|---|
| e<br>dress | ə<br>the<br>(shwa) | ɜ:<br>nurse | ɔ:<br>thought | ʊə<br>cure | ɔɪ<br>choice | əʊ<br>goat |
| æ<br>trap | ʌ<br>strut | ɑ:<br>start | ɒ<br>lot | eə<br>square | aɪ<br>price | aʊ<br>mouth |

### Consonants

| p<br>pip | b<br>bulb | t<br>tact | d<br>dared | tʃ<br>church | dʒ<br>judge | k<br>cake | g<br>gargle |
|---|---|---|---|---|---|---|---|
| f<br>fearful | v<br>vivid | θ<br>three | ð<br>this | s<br>cease | z<br>zones | ʃ<br>sheep | ʒ<br>treasure |
| m<br>mummy | n<br>nanny | ŋ<br>sing | h<br>hope | l<br>lull | r<br>red | w<br>went | j<br>yacht |